Fit for Eternal Life

Also available from
Sophia Institute Press®
by Kevin Vost:

Memorize the Faith

Kevin Vost, Psy.D.

Fit for Eternal Life

A Christian Approach to
Working Out,
Eating Right, and
Building the Virtues of Fitness
in Your Soul

SOPHIA INSTITUTE PRESS®
Manchester, New Hampshire

Copyright © 2007 Kevin Vost

Printed in the United States of America

All rights reserved

Cover design by Theodore Schluenderfritz

No part of this book may be reproduced, stored in a retrieval system, or transmitted in any form, or by any means, electronic, mechanical, photocopying, or otherwise, without the prior written permission of the publisher, except by a reviewer, who may quote brief passages in a review.

Sophia Institute Press®
Box 5284, Manchester, NH 03108
1-800-888-9344
www.sophiainstitute.com

Library of Congress Cataloging-in-Publication Data

Vost, Kevin.
    Fit for eternal life : a Christian approach to working
    out, eating right, and building the virtues of fitness in
    your soul / by Kevin Vost.
        p. cm.
    ISBN 978-1-933184-31-9 (pbk. : alk. paper)
    1. Physical fitness — Religious aspects — Christianity.
    I. Title.

BV4598.V67 2007
248.4 — dc22

                              2007038622

07 08 09 10 11 12 9 8 7 6 5 4 3 2 1

"He has shown strength with his arm."

Luke 1:51

To Kathy Ann (Collins) Vost:
a young lady of beautiful form
and sweetness of soul,
whom I met at the gym
in the Spring of '83

Contents

Part I
Body, Mind, and Spirit

Part II
The Strength of Fortitude:
Principles of Strength Training

Acknowledgments

This book would be mostly blank if I had been unable to draw upon the wisdom of the unlikely collection of philosophers, theologians, exercise theorists, and nutrition experts you'll meet in the pages ahead. My task is merely to help you literally "flesh" out their ideas in stronger muscles, sturdier bones, more powerful hearts, and more devout souls.

On a personal level, I can't thank enough all of the men and women who over the years have come under my guidance as a weightlifting teacher, fitness instructor, or training partner. This book would not be possible without your sufferings (and, I hope, your results).

Many thanks also to Todd Aglialoro of Sophia Institute Press®. He surprised me when he suggested a book on physical and spiritual fitness only weeks after I'd begun collecting my thoughts (and quotations) for just such a mind/body tome. His skill and patience in seeing this book through to a finished product did not surprise me.

Author's Note

We want you to be fit for eternal life, not to get there before your time! The information in this book is intended for healthy men and women. But even people without known health problems should consult their physician before starting any new exercise or dietary program. The material in this book is not a substitute for the advice of a personal healthcare professional. Any application of the advice in this book is at the reader's sole discretion and risk. The author and publisher disclaim any liability, personal, professional, or otherwise, resulting from the application or misapplication of the suggestions in this book.

Foreword

"Be Perfect"

*"Do you not know that your body is a temple
of the Holy Spirit within you, which you have from
God? You are not your own; you were bought
with a price. So glorify God in your body."*
I Corinthians 6:19

*"You, therefore, must be perfect,
as your heavenly Father is perfect."*
Matthew 5:48

*"The Church, without any doubt whatever, approves
of physical culture, if it be in proper proportion."*
Pope Pius XII

Since you've picked up this book, I suspect that you are already someone striving for spiritual perfection. Thank God for that. But meanwhile, have you let your body fall into a state of disrepair?

Perhaps you've become too accustomed to swimming against the current of our modern world, with its vain and superficial glorification of physical appearance. Or maybe work and family obligations have just left you too busy to get to the gym.

Or, maybe you've been putting so much focus on things spiritual that your body has gone neglected. After all, why should we waste time wrapping our hands around a barbell when we could be folding them in prayer? Shouldn't we be whipping our bodies, rather than whipping them into shape?

Not according to St. Paul. In his letter to the Corinthians, he tells us to treat the body as the Temple of the Holy Spirit, and to glorify God with it. God gave us our body as a most precious gift, and it is our Christian duty to care for it — indeed, to *perfect* it. In so doing, we show due reverence to the Holy Spirit who dwells within.

Of course, the modern world usually errs in the opposite extreme: treating the body as a god rather than as the dwelling-place of God. Physical indulgence and pleasure reign. But pious souls need not leave the world of the body to the hedonists. Yes, spiritual things are higher, but God made us beings of *both body and spirit*, now and for eternity. We are "ashes to ashes, dust to dust," it's true, but please recall: at the end of time, we are to be resurrected, soul *and* body.

The Glorified Body

That's surely why, in his *Summa Theologica*, St. Thomas Aquinas (the saint most closely connected to things of the *mind*) spends dozens of pages examining scriptural, traditional, and philosophical insights regarding the nature of our glorified body. He gives reasoned answers to all kinds of questions, from whether we will all arise with bodies of the same age and stature, to whether we will have internal organs, hair, and nails!

In Question 84 to the Supplement of the *Summa Theologica*, "On the Agility of the Bodies of the Blessed," St. Thomas writes:

> [T]he glorified body will be altogether subject to the glorified soul, so that not only will there be nothing in it to resist the will of the spirit, for it was even so in the case of Adam's body, but also from the glorified soul there will flow into the body a certain perfection, whereby it will become adapted to that subjection: and this perfection is called *the gift of the glorified body*.

In our glorified state, our bodies will fully obey the dictates of our spirits, unlike in our present state, where all too often the spirit is willing, but the flesh is weak. Without this interior conflict, our very bodily movements will become fluid, agile, and effortless.

But we don't have to wait for heaven to enjoy greater harmony between body and soul. St. Thomas also writes that "those in whom the motive power is stronger, and *those who through exercise have the body more adapted to obey the moving spirit*, labor less in being moved" (italics added). There are exercises, both physical and spiritual, that we can employ in *this* life, to make our body more completely subject to the rule of the soul, as well as more powerful and effective, more agile in its movements, and more beautiful in its form. Indeed, perfecting our bodies through proper dietary and exercise habits may prove a very apt earthly preparation for the glorified body of the resurrection.

Followers of Christ, you see, are not like St. Thomas's great nemesis the Manichees, who taught that the flesh itself is evil. Jesus himself took on human flesh in the Incarnation and thereby glorified it. Jesus came not to destroy the body, if you will, but to fulfill it. He showed us the way to perfection of our entire being, which includes our physical bodies — bones, sinews, and all.

Muscular Christianity and a Muscular Christ

The New Testament does not preach much directly about the value of sensible diet and exercise, but their value is there in principle, and through example. For instance, close your eyes and try to imagine the physical characteristics of Jesus Christ himself. He must have been magnificently fit and strong. The Virgin Mary herself nursed him and then helped establish his eating habits. Being free of sin, his dietary practices would have been guided by perfect temperance. His earthly father, St. Joseph, a hardworking carpenter, was the young Jesus' earthly model for physical strength and endurance. And Jesus himself, working without modern power tools, would undoubtedly have developed lean, powerful muscles. After he had begun his public ministry, we can barely read a chapter of the Gospels without hearing about his long journeys, mostly on foot, over hilly, unpaved paths. In his humanity, he would not have had the stamina to carry out his exhausting public work had he been in anything less than peak physical shape.

We find diet lessons too. Much ink in nutritional circles today has been devoted to touting the health and longevity benefits of the so-called "Mediterranean diet," some characteristics of which — such as bread, fish, olives, figs, wine, and water — will surely sound familiar to readers of Scripture. And who can forget those miracles wherein Jesus made wine from water and multiplied the loaves and fishes? If we are to be true imitators of Christ, shouldn't we also pay at least a little attention to how he sustained and used his bodily strength and endurance?

Further, we know that true Christian living is a matter not only of belief, but of action. St. James tells us clearly that "faith apart from works is dead."[1] What kind of works? The Church has for centuries preached two kinds of "works of mercy," one spiritual and the other corporal (or bodily). The corporal works of mercy remind us of those important needs of the body. We are to feed the hungry, give drink to the thirsty, clothe the naked, provide shelter for the homeless, and more. When we do these things for others, we do them for Christ himself.[2]

Modern exercise theorist (and Nautilus-machine inventor) Arthur Jones has noted that the muscles are the body's engines; therefore, they're also the engines of corporal works of mercy, since *our muscles are the movers that make those charitable actions physically possible.* The more powerful we make those engines, the more horses we'll have under the hood to do those powerful acts of good.

Papal Blessings for Physical Culture

Please take a second glance at the words of Pope Pius XII that grace the beginning of this foreword. He made that statement in 1948. Perhaps you've never heard the term *physical culture,* or you think it has an archaic ring, but I'd like to see it make a resurgence. *Culture* derives from the Latin word *cultura,* referring to tilling of the land. In the process of agricultural cultivation, man sets up

---

[1] Jas. 2:26.
[2] Matt. 25:31-46.

special conditions to improve the soil and enhance the growth of crops. Perfection in agricultural growth requires a delicate balance, a golden mean of water and sunshine and nutrients in the soil. So, too, does the concept of *physical culture* imply a careful, reasoned perfection of our physical selves. It implies in itself the criterion of "proper proportion."

What exactly did Pope Pius XII (a most athletic pontiff who had a gymnasium installed in the Vatican) mean by *proper proportion*? He said that exercise remains in proper proportion when it:

- does not lead to worship of the body;

- strengthens and energizes the body rather than draining it;

- provides refreshment for the spirit;

- does not lead to spiritual sloth or crudeness;

- provides "new excitements" for study and work; and

- does not disturb the peace and sanctity of the home.

Physical culture, then, is a wonderful thing when it brings us closer to bodily perfection, to spiritual renewal, to vocational achievement, and to health and harmony within our homes. It is anathema when it becomes a god to us — an end rather than a means. We must avoid the pitfalls of overweening self-pride and vanity, and of judgmental attitudes toward those who do not practice healthy lifestyles. We must avoid becoming so overly wrapped in the things of the body that we ignore the spirit it encloses.

It's critical to note, however, that attending to the needs of our body's perfection does not inevitably lead us to those vices. On the contrary, the cultivation of physical fitness can and should go hand in hand with the cultivation of moral virtue. *Physical culture and spiritual culture were literally made for each other — by God himself!*

Another great pontiff, Pope John Paul II, urged the world to have greater appreciation for the *theology of the body*, for a deeper understanding of the place of our physicality, sensuality, and sexuality in God's grand scheme of the universe. I think the time is right for a "theology of body*building*," as well: for greater appreciation and deeper understanding of the body's capacity for strength, endurance, and robust fitness, to serve as a dynamo of charity toward our neighbor and for the greater glory of God.

Introduction

Confessions of an
Iron-Pumping Psychologist

Who am I to talk about fitness, be it for this life or the next? That's a fair enough question.

What I'm not is a professional theologian, let alone a theological innovator. I'm a layman, just a guy sitting in the pew (and occasionally standing behind the lectern), trying to be faithful to Christ and his teachings. But although I'm very much a theological amateur, I do try to borrow my ideas from the very best of the professionals — especially St. Thomas Aquinas, the Universal Doctor himself. Also, I do have two areas of expertise that target physical and spiritual fitness within their crosshairs.

First, I've been involved in the fields of weightlifting and fitness training for almost forty years now. The first time I ever saw a lifter on television, when I was but in the second grade at age seven or eight, I implored my parents to buy me a barbell set, and happily, they complied. In fact, to this day, my own sons use some of the same old, red, plastic, sand-filled discs. Those old barbell plates still bear the duct tape my boys' grandfather used to patch them in the 1960s, so that no precious grains of muscle-bestowing sand would be lost as I put myself through my exercises.

In my teens, I was quite obsessed with the worlds of muscle-building and fitness training, at a time right before they moved from being a quirky subculture to a widely popular and visible part of the mainstream. My training became a regular habit that persists to this day. I went on to compete in bodybuilding, in Olympic-style weightlifting, and in power lifting, not to mention such sideshows as ten-man tug-of-war teams and team human tractor-pulling competitions. In seven years of competition, I went from a 135-pound teenager doing a clean and jerk with 165 pounds to a 205-pound young adult, benching 400 pounds, and squatting and deadlifting over 550.

I also worked my way through college as a weightlifting instructor at a YMCA and at two fitness centers, immersing myself in the muscle-building literature of the 1960s through the 1980s (and eventually collecting several bins of well-worn books and magazines). My lifting buddies and I traveled all around the Midwest, attending contests and seminars featuring the era's greatest bodybuilders.

Later, in my thirties and early forties, I branched out into endurance activities such as running, but I stayed involved in strength sports through Scottish Highland Games competitions: heaving and tossing cabers (tree trunks), 56-pound iron balls, hammers, hay bales, and large stones (all while clad in a kilt, no less). Then, in the late Nineties, I also began writing fitness and sports-psychology articles for websites and magazines.

In recent years, I have kept up my learning in the field, seeking personalized guidance through the late Mike Mentzer, a brilliant former Mr. Universe who was at one time bodybuilding's heir-apparent to Arnold Schwarzenegger, and from Clarence Bass, a former Olympic weightlifting champion, over-forty Mr. USA winner, and current master in the fields of total fitness and leanness.

My special focus within the field of exercise science is something called High-Intensity Training, or HIT. This is a system of strength training that produces maximum results in strength and muscle tone from a minimal investment of time. I will tell you all about it in the pages ahead!

Confessions of an Iron-Pumping Psychologist

Over the course of my nearly forty years of involvement in the world of fitness, I'm pretty sure I've learned a lot of important things, and I'm absolutely certain that I've made a boatload of mistakes. I hope to help you benefit at least as much from my mistakes as from my knowledge!

Mind over Matter:
The Psychology of Physical Perfection

My other area of expertise? I'm also a Doctor of Psychology in Clinical Psychology. (That's what the "Psy.D." means.) I think that in fitness training, knowledge is only half the story, because it's one thing to know *what* to do, but another thing to know *how to get yourself to do it!*

That's where psychology can help. To become truly fit, healthful exercise and eating behaviors must become *habitual*. Habits must build upon human nature, and part of psychology's job is to help us understand our human nature, both its potential and its limitations.

Most people fail in their efforts to attain a total fitness lifestyle because they hold unrealistic expectations about what diet and exercise can do for them, and about their abilities to change their own behaviors. We might get fired up to get in shape because of a scary cholesterol-screening result, or just because our pants button explodes from the sheer force of the protruding waistline beneath it, yet whatever the motivation might be, if our exercise program doesn't produce the desired results, we won't be able to maintain it.

But, drawing on psychological knowledge about human nature, and the potential capacities of our own intellects, desires, and wills, we discover that we are best able to stick with exercise and diet programs and see long-term results when we:

- grasp the logic of the basic interrelated principles of exercise and diet, and how to adapt them to our own needs and life routines;

- understand the principles of habit formation and realize that acquiring good habits means acquiring virtues;

- train ourselves to desire and obtain a feeling of accomplishment (and fun) from our exercise programs;

- acquire the self-discipline of will to seek small positive results in the short run (virtually every workout for strength-training sessions for months to come);

- learn how to enjoy our daily diets, thinking neither too much nor too little about our daily bread;

- obtain the peace of mind and fortitude of will that comes from the realization that God wants us to perfect our human natures — soul, mind, *and body.*

These things are more easily talked about than done, but they *can* be done. (Near the end of the book, I'll cap off my "confessions" by showing you how it wasn't until the age of forty-five that I really began to put those points together myself.) And by the time we're through, you'll have all the tools and knowledge you'll need to do it.

KISS: Keep it Simple, Samson

St. Thomas had a great gift for making the complex simple and understandable, and in these pages, I will try to do likewise. For I believe that physical fitness and diet have become needlessly overcomplicated. Even in a short book like this one you *can* find enough guidance in the fundamentals to get your body in good working order, without having to earn a doctorate in exercise physiology or nutrition first. It will take a fair measure of effort, sweat, and perseverance, to be sure, but it will all be simple, straightforward, and commonsensical. Let's get to it!

Fit for Eternal Life

Part I

Body, Mind, and Spirit

"But if a man uses exercise, food, and drink in moderation, he will become physically strong and his health will be improved and preserved. It is the same with the virtues of the soul — for instance, fortitude, temperance, and the other virtues."
St. Thomas Aquinas

Chapter 1

Introducing Total Fitness

"There is a need to find free time in order to exercise strength and dexterity, endurance, and harmonious movement, so as to attain or guarantee that physical efficiency necessary to man's overall equilibrium."
Pope John Paul II

"The highest merit should not be attributed to him who has the strongest and most agile muscles, but rather to him who shows the most ready ability in keeping them subject to the power of the spirit."
Pope Pius XII

This book is about building your temple, both inside and out. It is about perfecting yourself as a being created in God's image. It is written in such a way that if you read along carefully, eat right, and get enough sleep, you will be well on your way to understanding the fundamental principles of physical fitness and applying them to your daily life — for the rest of your life. Even more, you'll learn to view total physical fitness within the broader and overarching context of a *truly* *total* fitness in which the body takes its rightful place in harmony with the mind and spirit: a fitness to prepare you for *eternal* life.

Psyching Up: Virtues and the Habits of Fitness

Countless books have been written about strength training and diet in the last few decades alone. They gleam from their places on bookstore shelves, but when purchased, most have been destined to gather dust on our own shelves (perhaps not far from that exercise bike/clothing hanger gathering its own dust in the corner). But this isn't always our fault; too often, the advice these books give is inconsistent, inefficient, ineffective, incomplete, and impractical.

What you need instead are techniques for training and feeding your body that are practically achievable — techniques you can comfortably and enjoyably incorporate into your daily routines. In short, you need to be shown how to make fitness a good habit: a *virtue*. This is our first goal.

Pumping Up:
The Components of Total Physical Fitness

Next we will examine the actual principles for strength training, endurance training, and diet. Strength training will come first and will lay its rightful claim to the lion's share of ink. Too many fitness books overvalue cardiovascular endurance or "aerobic" training — at strength training's expense. But our Temple of the Holy Spirit must not be built on sand, and it is strength training, not aerobics, that will provide it with a rock-like foundation of powerful muscles, ligaments, tendons, and bones. Over the course of seven chapters on interrelated strength-training principles, you'll be given a firm foundation in the skills and know-how for firming your own foundation. But don't worry: no temple divided against itself can stand, so I'll still give endurance training and diet their rightful due in the chapters that follow.

Since there's so much to the fields of exercise and nutrition (let alone the psychology and theology of virtue and fitness), a small book such as this can cover only the basics. Still, at the end of each chapter, I've added boxes with specialized additional information. These "Muscle Mastery Tips and Facts" will include advanced training techniques, suggestions for further reading, ways to derive spiritual benefits from physical endeavors, and more. Just keep reading and you'll see what I mean.

The Simple and Intense Path to Fitness

But make no mistake: the fundamentals alone can carry you a long, long way. This is one of the most important ideas I'd like you to remember: *fitness training in general, and especially strength training in particular, are really rather simple and straightforward in their basic principles.* As you'll see in the chapters to come, strength training is really more like "rock science" than "rocket science."

Fitness instructors often forget this. They can guide you through the proper set-up and performance of an exercise on a given piece of equipment, but they often have little knowledge or firsthand experience with the system of High Intensity Training (HIT) that I'll detail in these pages. HIT, which has been around since the 1960s, is especially advantageous for people who desire to live full lives (outside the gym!), because it entails brief, intense, and infrequent training that can require as little as *twenty minutes in one weekly session*. It's both safe and effective, with rationally consistent guidelines applicable to men and women of all ages.

I'll also simplify aerobic exercise, giving you guidelines for a basic, but effective, cardiovascular training regimen involving as little as *three twenty-minute sessions a week*. (And in case you can't spare even that much time, in chapter 11, I'll show you how to render those sessions completely optional.)

Diet is also essential to total health and fitness. It holds the ultimate key to weight control and healthy leanness. And — you guessed it — it's another area that has been made far too complicated by diet experts and trainers. Instead of counting every carb, we're going to focus on the virtue of *temperance* as it relates to diet. For gluttony — temperance's foe — can bloat, distort, and weaken our bodily temples, and like any vice, it diverts our attention from things of the spirit; it leaves us unfit for both this life and the next. That's why practical advice on sensible eating (and how to get yourself to stick with it) will be our food for thought in part IV.

The Virtues of Becoming Your Own Personal Trainer

By the time we reach part V, we'll be ready to start putting together routines that incorporate strength training, formal aerobic training, and normal physical activities, as well as healthy dietary practices to last a lifetime. You'll begin to practice the virtues of fitness. You'll have begun to acquire the tools to become *your own physical trainer*!

By this point, we will have seen time and again that the kinds of "muscular virtues" that lead to total physical fitness are a matter of *knowledge, will,* and *daily practice.* We will see that attaining total fitness is a matter of both *knowing what to do* and *knowing how to get yourself to do it.* Near the end, therefore, we'll concentrate on motivation and encouragement, focused on attaining real results in perfection of body and soul and enjoying the process along the way.

Beyond Human Virtue and Fitness: Fit for *Eternal* Life

In every chapter, we will examine the best methods that modern reason, science, and technology have crafted for the perfection of our bodies; we will give a nod to the insights from classical philosophy; and we will consider how this all bears on a theology of bodily fitness that treats that body as a temple of the Holy Spirit, and seeks to *perfect* it in response to God's commandment. By the conclusion, we'll be prepared to give the spiritual its full and rightful due by emphasizing how all this training in virtue is animated by three special virtues: faith, hope, and charity. These God-infused virtues are the ultimate foundation on which to build our bodily temples of the Holy Spirit, and the ultimate goal to which they are ordered.

Fitness for Every Body

But wait. There's more! In the appendix, we'll try to do *justice*, by duly addressing the special needs and concerns of some particular groups: women, older persons, and teens.

Although every woman is an individual with her own unique concerns, women as a group do tend to have several common fitness concerns (few are interested in developing the rippling bi-ceps their teenage sons are seeking, yet many want to improve their appearance and energy levels). Women will also have to deal with special fitness issues as they age, such as the loss of bone mass.

And speaking of aging, both women and men in their golden years will benefit from the proper kind of physical training. Mod-ern studies demonstrate that a good measure of the decline in strength, muscle mass, and cardiovascular endurance we typically suffer with age is to some extent preventable and reversible. We'll look at some of those research studies and include some practical recommendations for attaining or maintaining *your* physical peak throughout your life span.

As for those teens and their goal of rippling biceps, sadly, the advice they find in modern muscle magazines is rarely conducive to bodily health, let alone mental and spiritual growth. Teenage boys are constantly bombarded today with the message that "big-ger is better" (by most any means necessary), while girls are fed a media diet extolling just the opposite: an impossibly slim body im-age that is unrealistic, unattainable, and often dangerous. Teens absorb these messages precisely at the time of their lives when they should be establishing diet and fitness habits to prepare them for a lifetime of health and vigor. But at their age, they often lack the knowledge and experience to separate the wheat from the chaff.

So then, are you ready to get fit — fit for *eternal* life? If you're ready to make your body thrive, and not just survive, and not to neglect it, but to perfect it, if you're starting to get psyched and pumped, then let's begin: as with any good workout, by warm-ing up.

MUSCLE MASTERY TIPS AND FACTS #1

Caveat Flexor

Perhaps Latinists, or those who have studied economics, will recognize the phrase *caveat emptor* — "let the buyer beware" (lest he be bamboozled)! Well, those who would become *flexors* (exercisers) should keep some *caveats* (forewarnings) in mind. This book is not intended to replace your doctor's medical advice. Check with your doctor before embarking on any rigorous exercise program. We will strive to become fit for *eternal* life, but we don't want to start the eternal part prematurely.

Chapter 2

The Virtues of Fitness

*"Virtue, inasmuch as it is a suitable disposition
of the soul, is like health and beauty, which
are suitable dispositions of the body."*
St. Thomas Aquinas

*"Every virtue or excellence puts into good condition
that of which it is a virtue or excellence, and
enables it to perform its work well."*
Aristotle

"To achieve excellence, we first must sweat."
Hesiod

All of us know firsthand that we are beings of both matter and spirit, "ensouled bodies." The *Catechism of the Catholic Church* elaborates that "the unity of soul and body is so profound that one has to consider the soul to be the 'form' of the body . . . spirit and matter in man are not two natures united, but rather their union forms a single nature."[3] If you'd care for a fine and fancy term for this unity, long ago Aristotle referred to it as *hylomorphism* — *hyle* meaning "matter" and *morphe* meaning "form."

Philosophers such as old Aristotle argued that striving to be the best that we can be in body and soul is also what leads us to happiness. Jesus echoed the ancient philosophers when he commanded his followers to "be perfect." The word *perfect* derives from the Latin for "complete." Given our body-soul natures, it follows that we must strive to be perfect according to our entire nature: soul *and* body. Now, this doesn't mean we must spend our time and energies obsessing about attaining "the body perfect" — any more than we should become paralyzed with scrupulosity as we attempt to perfect our souls. Rather, we are to try to perfect the form and functions of our bodies *within their natural limitations.*

Setting Fallen Bodies Aright

For who among us is not aware of his body's limits? We're reminded most every day (especially if we're over forty!) how the

---

[3] *Catechism of the Catholic Church* (CCC), par. 365.

Fall made us prone not only to sin, but also to physical weakness and pain.

As we learn from the first chapter of the book of Genesis, prior to the sin of Adam and Eve, there was no toil, no fatigue, and no death. But after our first parents disobeyed God, they not only lost eternal friendship with him, but the human body "fell" into a state subject to disharmony, corruption, and decay. The flesh no longer obeyed the spirit. For the rest of time, human beings would experience labor pains, backaches, arthritis, cancers — and finally, the grave.

This condition is an ever-present obstacle in our efforts to achieve total fitness. If we still enjoyed complete harmony of body and soul, no special discipline or self-restraint would be required to eat right and exercise regularly. Virtues would come easily, rather than with sweat and sacrifice. As St. Thomas told us, the body would be completely agile, its actions and movements flowing effortlessly from the guidance of the spirit.

When we reach our ultimate destiny — our glorified physical state in heaven — we will no longer have to deal with pain or weakness; neither will we have to contend with gluttony, lust, intemperance, sloth, or any of the multitude of vices with which we do battle in our fallen state of disordered will and appetites. But in the meantime, here on earth we must nonetheless seek to perfect our bodies and souls, fallen though they are.

How is this to be achieved?

Well, to start, we must try, by God's grace, to re-establish some harmony between body and soul, and between our reason, and will, and sensual appetites. This *cultivation of virtue* will allow us to combat weakness and overcome the discouragement of pain, restoring to some degree the hylomorphic harmony upon which fitness depends.

The Nature of Virtue

The *Catechism of the Catholic Church* addresses the virtues in its section on "Life in Christ,"[4] because virtues guide us in living good lives as Christians. But the natural or human virtues have been a subject in both pagan and Christian writings for millennia. In his thirteenth-century writings, St. Thomas Aquinas synthesized them most thoroughly and elevated them most sublimely, particularly in the *Summa Theologica*.

The word *virtue* derives from the Latin word *vir*, for "man." Virtues, then, allow us to become more fully and perfectly human, by *disposing us to perform good acts, to perfect ourselves, and to give the best of ourselves*. When we possess the virtues, it becomes more natural, easy, and enjoyable for us to do the right things. We're able to maximize our human powers.

Those fundamental powers include the abilities to *desire* and to *will*, to discern what we seek to enjoy or to avoid, and to choose freely whether we will pursue those desires. Since our natures are fallen, our desires by themselves are no sure guides to excellence and happiness.

This is as true for physical fitness as it is for the moral life. Just look at what sedentary living and the pursuit of super-size junk-food meals has done to the bodies of so many citizens in our affluent nation.

No, to exercise virtue, our desires and choices must be guided by *reason* (and for Christians, of course, by our *faith* as well). This perfection of our thinking, desiring, and choosing is the stuff of the virtues, those peaks of excellence that crown our human natures and point us toward total fitness and, ultimately, toward heaven.

[4] Par. 1803-1845.

The Virtues of Nature

As we pursue total spiritual and physical fitness within these pages, we will address and employ seven fundamental virtues. The first four are called natural or human virtues — those virtues recognized first by the great pagan philosophers. The seeds of these virtues are inborn in our human nature, and they can thrive or wither through our own efforts or lack thereof. They help us counteract and conquer the vices that arise from the sinful side of our fallen nature.

These four virtues are also known as "moral" virtues, because they pertain to *doing* good (the "intellectual" virtues, on the other hand, first help us to *know* what is good). These virtues are:

Prudence

Fortitude

Temperance

Justice

Some might call prudence "practical wisdom," fortitude "courage" or "strength" or "endurance," and temperance "self-control" or "moderation." I don't think justice has picked up a new moniker, which seems fair enough to me. (Okay, maybe "fairness.")

Prudence, fortitude, temperance, and justice have been historically known as the "cardinal" virtues, based on the Latin word *cardo* meaning "the hinge of a door." For all other virtues hinge on them, swing from them, and can't operate fully without them. As Scripture tells us, "And if anyone loves righteousness, her labors are virtues: for she teaches self-control and prudence, justice and courage; nothing in life is more profitable for men than these."[5]

---

[5] Wisd. 8:7.

This reads to me like true wisdom indeed. So let's use the cardinal virtues as a framework for the parts of this book. The virtue of fortitude entails strength and endurance despite bodily discomfort — what an apt virtue for addressing the toils of strength training and cardiovascular training. Temperance, or self-control, works just as obviously in the service of regulating our daily diet. Justice consists of giving all their rightful due. We'll do this when we address the fitness needs of special groups.

Last is prudence, the practical wisdom to act in accordance with right reason. This is a unique blend of "intellectual" and "moral" virtue, for it requires both *knowing* what is right and *acting* on that knowledge. It's about applying general principles in specific situations, about finding the proper means to virtuous ends. It's about getting the job done! The *Catechism* notes that prudence has been called the *auriga virtutum*, the "charioteer of the virtues"[6] — that which steers them to their ends.

In part V of this book, prudence will grab the reins to drive us home as we apply the principles of fitness training to our own practical situations — creating our own successful programs for total fitness.

What the Golden Mean . . . Means

Aristotle's conception of virtue has been called "the golden mean," and we'll be seeing a lot of that idea in the pages ahead. "Nothing in excess" was a related Greek maxim. It means that virtue lies between the vices of extremes, between deficiency on one side and excess on the other.

But perhaps the mean or the middle also conveys to you the suggestion of mediocrity. Should we be virtuous, then, but not *too*

[6] CCC, par. 1806.

virtuous? No, the mean does not mean going halfway. Aristotle would not have us be the lukewarm who will be spit out![7] The golden mean at which the cardinal virtues aim is not compromise *between* virtue and vice; rather it is a golden peak of excellence that towers *above* deficiency and excess. As we pursue fitness, total fitness, *virtuous fitness*, we will keep our eyes fixed upon this golden peak at all times.

Psyched and Pumped: Building the Habits of Physical and Moral Excellence

So how do we get these virtues? The answer lies in their very definition.

Every virtue is a kind of habit, and "a habit is a disposition whereby that which is disposed is disposed well or ill, and this, either in regard to itself or in regard to another; thus health is a habit."[8] In more modern language, virtues are *habitual patterns of thought and behavior* that dispose a person to the proper use of his powers.

And how do we acquire virtuous patterns of behavior? *By the performance of virtuous actions.* It's Aristotle's turn now. As he said in Book I of his *Nichomachean Ethics*:

> We become builders by building and harpists by playing the harp. Similarly, it is by doing just acts that we become just, by doing temperate acts that we become temperate, by doing brave acts that we become brave.

This might seem for a second like a chicken-and-egg situation. In order to perform virtuous actions, wouldn't we already have to

[7] Rev. 3:16.
[8] *Summa Theologica (ST)*, I-II, Q. 49, art. 1.

20

be virtuous? Partially, but not entirely. How does a weightlifter acquire the strength to lift enormous weights? He starts by lifting much lighter weights, and then uses progressively heavier weights over time as he becomes stronger and stronger. He starts with the muscles that nature provided him; *then* he perfects them through his habitual actions. (Stay tuned next chapter for an explanation of how this actually works in strength training.)

Nature has provided us all with the necessary initial dispositions to virtue. We all have appetites or passions, reason, and will. Now, what are we going to *do* with them? To turn them into habitual inclinations toward the good (i.e., into virtues), we must perform virtuous acts again and again and again. As St. Thomas put it, "A disposition becomes a habit, just as a boy becomes a man."[9]

As you perform the actions that lead to the physical or "muscular" virtues of strength, endurance, and leanness, it will become progressively easier to stay at your physical peak. As you acquire the discipline and expertise that come with habitual training, you'll even find that your actual workouts become more pleasurable. This works at both the neurological and psychological levels — a way for our muscles to provide us with an immediate and tangible reward for a job well done.

Aerobic exercise offers similar rewards. Efforts that might at first seem like torture (especially if you attempt too much too soon), will soon seem like a walk in the park. And even if a simple "walk in the park" sounds rather laborious to you right now, well, you can start with a walk around the block. (And you might even want to bring along a friend, to talk.)

There are other very beneficial side effects (apart from their intended ends) of virtues in general, both spiritual and "muscular"

---

[9] *ST*, I-II, Q. 49, art. 2.

virtues. *Virtues, when developed, make it easier for us to make the right choices.* When the virtues compatible with fitness exist in us as deeply ingrained habits, healthy choices, both in the gym and at the table, will become "second nature" and almost automatic. Further, we should never forget that "happiness is the reward of virtue."[10] Let's move along then and get ready to build some rippling muscles (and rippling virtues) as we dig into part II, the principal principles of building bodily strength (and moral fortitude along the way).

[10] *ST*, I-II, Q. 57, art. 1.

MUSCLE MASTERY TIPS AND FACTS #2

Strength Training:
The Stronger You Get, the Less You Need
This one is really good news! In traditional strength-training systems, beginners are advised to begin with two or three sets — groups of repetitions — per exercise and to advance to four or five as time goes by (and to add more exercises as well). That means the stronger you get, the *more* time you'll have to spend in the gym to improve. How exciting a prospect for those of us with other things to do! But the truth is really quite the opposite when you come to appreciate the interplay between the principles of intensity, duration, frequency, and rest as you'll see in the chapters ahead. In a nutshell, the more powerful your muscles become, the more taxing each set becomes on your capacity to rebuild and recuperate. So, as you become stronger with time, you will *not* need more than one set per exercise; you will require workouts with *fewer* total exercises, and you may wait *longer* between workouts. A strong muscle is a well-rested, efficient, and happy muscle!

Part II

The Strength of Fortitude: Principles of Strength Training

"Virtue implies a perfection of power . . .
Every evil is a weakness."
St. Thomas Aquinas

Chapter 3

Progression Toward Perfection

"And may the Lord make you increase . . ."
1 Thessalonians 3:2

"And if you are accustomed to doing this,
you will see what shoulders, what muscles,
what strength you have."
Epictetus

The ancient Greeks told the story of the Father of Weightlifting, or more properly stated, the Father of "Progressive Resistance Training." His name was Milo of Croton (c. 557-500 BC). Just imagine this young lad of the Greek colony of Croton on the island of Syracuse, off the southern coast of Italy, lifting a small calf, day after day. As the calf grows into a bull, so, too, does Milo grow, into a mighty bull of a man! By age seventeen, he is ready to don his laurel wreath as Olympic wrestling champion, a title he will defend for the next three decades (at least once going uncontested with no willing combatants). He also studies philosophy as a follower of Pythagoras (yes, the geometry-theorem guy). Milo's legendary physique and power stir the imaginations of the mind- and body-loving ancient Greeks. This is no rotund modern super heavyweight, but a veritable Hercules on earth!

Indeed, one story tells of Milo wielding an enormous club and donning a lion's skin overhead, like Hercules, leading a charging army of 100,000 Crotoniates to route a force of 300,000 Sybarites. Surely, sane Sybarites strove to move far from the thunderous blows of Milo's club, lest they suffer a fate like that of the thousand Philistines who came too close to the jawbone that Samson wielded. In the stadium at Olympia, Milo will delight in carrying a four-year-old heifer more than 500 yards, felling the animal with a single blow, then eating the whole carcass.

We will return to Milo later, but the fundamental principle that we draw from him here derives from that tale of his boyhood, of those daily workouts with a living, growing calf. It is the principle of *progression*, the necessity of placing the muscles under increasingly demanding loads to stimulate growth in size and strength. *Progression* is the first key to building muscular strength and size.

In a mature individual, muscles have no reason to grow except in response to demands placed upon them. Do you recall my saying that strength training its more like "rock science" than "rocket science"? Here is the principle again. To stimulate muscles to grow, we must provide them with increasing demands. We must challenge them to lift progressively heavier weights, whether rocks, calves, barbells, or the weight stacks or air resistance of high-tech strength-training machines.

Spiritual Progression

Those wise old Greeks understood the principle of progression more than two thousand years ago — at least as far as *physical* strength building goes. Of course, the Christian seeking perfection is also in earnest pursuit of *spiritual* progression. St. Paul uses *bodily* metaphors to address the necessity of spiritual progression in his first letter to the Corinthians (who happened to be Greeks): "I fed you with milk, not solid food; for you were not ready for it; and even yet you are not ready, for you are still of the flesh."[11] His teachings were adjusted to their limited spiritual understanding, so focused were they on things of this world. To produce spiritual growth, St. Paul directed them away from their earthly teachers and toward Jesus Christ as the ultimate foundation of the lives they were to build on earth, aiming toward their ultimate salvation.

And to aid them in their spiritual progress, St. Paul shared that idea which serves as our foundation for attaining total physical

[11] 1 Cor. 3:2-3.

and spiritual fitness. "Do you not know that you are God's temple and that God's Spirit dwells in you? If anyone destroys God's temple, God will destroy him. For God's temple is holy, and that temple you are."[12] Isn't the last line rather striking? *And that temple you are.* Now there's something to really think about — and act upon.

We can also see parallels of physical progression in the process of growth through the various stages of prayer, beginning with the initial rote recitation and memorization of standard formulas, then to deeper meditation on their meanings, and finally, in some cases, to the transcendent, wordless, mystical communication with God experienced by some great saints of exceptional spiritual fitness.

Progression in Fortitude

Fortitude derives from the Latin adjective *fortis*, meaning physically strong and sturdy. As a moral virtue, it implies strength of resolve, firmness, courage, and endurance. St. Thomas has called fortitude the "guardian" of the virtues. It prevents our reason from being overcome by physical pain or adversity. And as moral fortitude guards the integrity of virtues of our souls, so, too can physical strength help guard the integrity of our bodies.

Progress in physical strength may help give us the confidence to be more courageous in our moral actions, and progress in the virtue of fortitude can help us endure the discomfort of physical training that makes our muscles strong.

Progress, of course, is this chapter's theme. Shall we progress beyond Milo, then, and see how we've progressed in understanding progression?

[12] 1 Cor. 3:16-17.

The Double Progression Method Today

In strength training with weights or free weights, two forms of progression are performed — it's sometimes called the *"double progression method."* The first form of progression is the performance of additional repetitions with the same weight.[13]

For example, let's say you can do eight repetitions with fifty pounds on a barbell curl. Next workout, you would strive to perform nine or ten repetitions with that same weight. Once you had successfully completed twelve repetitions, a few workouts down the road, you would increase the poundage a bit, perhaps to fifty-five pounds. (That's the second progression.) You might then be reduced to eight or nine repetitions again, but you would strive over the next several workouts to achieve twelve repetitions in good form. Once that is accomplished, yes, you guessed it, time for a small increase in the poundage, and so it goes. Progression in number of *repetitions* with a particular weight (usually in the range of eight to twelve) followed by progression in *weight* lifted. To paraphrase from the instructions on shampoo bottles, rinse off the sweat, rest until next workout, repeat.

There is strength training, in a nutshell. If you can progress like this, within a year or two you could attain and then maintain your maximum strength levels, as well as your maximum muscle mass, depending on your sex and individual genetics. But such progression is not quite such a straightforward process. The other strength-training principles we'll discover in the chapters ahead are necessary to ensure that progression actually occurs. If, for example, your muscles are under-trained, over-trained, or strained, your strength

---

[13] When you perform the movement of a particular exercise once, it's called a *repetition*. A group of consecutive repetitions done without stopping is called a *set*. Sets and *repetitions* are among the basics of strength-training vocabulary.

could plateau, or even decline. It is all these principles taken together that really separate high-intensity training (HIT) from other conventional methods of strength training. They form a rational, interlocking system of ideas. They make sense, and they make muscle.

The Lord has given our bodies built-in mechanisms so that our muscles increase in response to exercise, but we must do our part. And if we do, to borrow from the wise old Stoic philosopher Epictetus (first century AD), lo, what strength and what shoulders shall we have, perhaps not sufficient to shoulder a bull, but surely sufficient to shoulder the burdens of everyday life!

MUSCLE MASTERY TIPS AND FACTS #3

Three Kinds of Muscular Strength

Skeletal muscles have three levels of strength, each capable of handling heavier resistance than the last, yet traditional forms of strength training tend to focus only on the first. In the *positive* or concentric portion of a repetition, the weight is raised while the muscles move from a stretched to a contracted state when the movement is completed. Positive motion is important, and strength training is called weight *lifting* after all. Still, you can gain strength more quickly if you pay attention to how you *lower* the weight. This is actually the third and most powerful function of our muscles — to safely resist a load as we lower it back to the starting position. This is called *negative* or eccentric strength. We can safely lower up to about 40 percent more weight than we can lift in a positive fashion. *Static* strength levels lie in between the two. Static strength refers to the ability to hold a weight motionless with muscles in the contracted position. There are special techniques to bring all three into play in your high-intensity strength training, giving every set you do an extra wallop. Stay tuned for the specifics in the next Muscle Mastery Tips and Facts box, coming to you soon.

Chapter 4

Intensity for Muscular Immensity

"My heart throbs, my strength fails me."
Psalm 38:10

*"If a man is a long-distance runner, there is a certain
kind of diet, walking, massage, and exercise. If someone is a sprinter, all these things are different. If he is
entering the pentathlon, they are even more different."*
Epictetus

When our local shopping mall celebrated its grand opening in 1977, one of the celebrities brought in to help was a man considered by many to be the world's greatest athlete (and to sport the ideal male physique as well). Any guesses?

All right, the athlete was Olympian decathlete Bruce Jenner. Why do I mention him? Take another peek at the quotation from the ancient Greek philosopher Epictetus at the beginning of this chapter. He is quite correct that physical training should be tailored to one's sport. The ancient pentathlon consisted of five events that required the athlete to run, throw a discus, throw a javelin, jump for distance, and wrestle, thus demonstrating a combination of strength, endurance, skill, and strategy. The modern decathlon involves ten events. Wrestling has gone by the wayside, but three more runs of varying distance and style, high jumping, pole vaulting, and shot putting have been added.

I realize there probably aren't many decathletes among my readers. But let the decathlon serve as our *symbolic* sport, since we're in training for the sport of life: this life and the life to come. St. Paul has already compared the Christian life to athletic training and competition, using both running and boxing as examples. To perfect ourselves, we must be versatile, brimming over with the strength, endurance, and agility to cope with whatever physical challenges are thrown our way. *So let us consider ourselves "decathletes" of physical and spiritual fitness.* That doesn't mean we'll be pole-vaulting over anything; it just reminds us that we will strive for *total* fitness involving well-rounded strength, as well as endurance.

Push Your Muscles to Their Limit

Intensity in strength training refers to how hard you're working, particularly to the percentage of "momentary muscular effort." Let's think back to the young Milo, lifting that calf. When both were little, Milo did a whole lot of huffing and puffing. His workout was intense. But what if Milo had continued growing, as a young boy is bound to do, but the calf stopped growing? Milo's daily round with that calf would have become progressively less intense and would have had progressively less effect on enhancing the normal rate of growth in his strength and muscular size. Intensity, then, is directly tied to progression. As muscles become progressively stronger, they must be put to harder and harder tests. They must be stimulated to grow with intense efforts commensurate with their current levels of strength.

Consider, for example, the leg press, an exercise wherein your back is supported by a cushioned pad and your feet rest against a moveable metal footrest connected to a stack of weights. You start with your knees back up near your chest and finish with your legs extended and knees nearly locked. If you can leg-press 200 pounds for ten repetitions in good form, why should the quadriceps muscles of your thighs grow if, during each workout, you come in and do the same weight for the same number of repetitions in the same manner? There would be no increase in intensity, no progression in resistance, and no muscle growth. Worse yet, suppose you decided to do only nine repetitions, or eight, or reduce the resistance to 180 pounds. This might even cause your muscles to shrink or atrophy, and your strength to decline, because the intensity would be diminished — a case perhaps of "progressive regression."

No, to build strength, intensity must remain high. Traditionally, High-Intensity Training has recommended maximizing intensity by training "to failure." In essence, if you stop at nine repetitions, this would mean that you attempted a tenth, but couldn't do it — that you failed to complete your last repetition because it exceeded your capacity. Training to failure in this manner is quite demanding, but it ensures that intensity stays high as can be.

Consider intensity also within a given set of an exercise. If you can do nine repetitions with a given weight, let's say 100 pounds, you could lift considerably more for just one repetition. Therefore, the first several repetitions of your set of 100 pounds are relatively easy — of low intensity for you. It is those last few difficult repetitions that become truly intense, and most of all, that *last one* that produces failure. But most conventional systems of strength training call for completion of some predetermined number of repetitions, none of which may bring you to a high level of intensity.

Now, it is *not* the case that 100-percent intensity is absolutely required to produce enough stimulation for muscle growth. Perhaps ninety-two will do it on a particular day — but we have no way of knowing exactly how much intensity is required for you, and no way of knowing how close you are until you hit failure. So training to failure ensures that you cross the growth-stimulation threshold.

Still, I'm not actually recommending that you *always* train to failure. Some very successful trainers and thoughtful proponents of the HIT philosophy (including Clarence Bass, whom we'll meet in the chapters ahead), advocate leaving just a little for the next workout. This would entail not failing entirely on one's last repetition, but coming close, sensing that the next repetition probably would lead to failure, thus leaving a little room for improvement the next time. I usually train that way myself. How do you know that you generated enough intensity to stimulate growth? You won't until the next workout. If you are indeed stronger, then you did something right the last time around.

Please note: you can't compensate for low-intensity training by doing a whole lot of it! Occasionally my weightlifting buddy and I will say to each other, "A little bit of something does more than a whole lot of nothing" as we observe this common workout practice in the gym. To our thinking, if you don't work hard enough to trigger muscle growth, if you're just tickling the muscles, then you're spinning your wheels, no matter how much time you put into it. (Not to mention, you're taking up space on the machine that might be put to good use by some hard-working HIT trainer!) Low-intensity training is like trying to get a suntan by lying all day under an ordinary light bulb. A few minutes of intense sunshine (with the proper sunscreen, of course) would certainly do more to bronze you up!

Firing Up Your Spiritual Dynamo

"I know your works," the Lord says. "You are neither cold nor hot. Would that you were cold or hot! So, because you are lukewarm, and neither cold nor hot, I will spew you out of my mouth."[14] God's Word commands us to make our good works burn with spiritual intensity, not merely to go through the motions. We do not grow spiritually through half-measures, nor do we make our bodies stronger that way. In both areas, we should act with a tireless and loving boldness.

The American psychologist William James, a pioneer in the study of habit formation, said that we usually go through life only half-alive, half-awake, with "our fires half-damped," unless some

[14] Rev. 3:16.

"dynamogenic idea" serves to wake us up and stoke our flames. There is our fallen human nature again. We naturally tend toward leisure and easy pleasures, being satisfied with a lame mediocrity. But true physical progress, like spiritual progress, is made through radical self-giving, through seeking out difficult challenges. It is intensity that leads to muscular immensity. If you are stingy with your physical efforts in the gym, your body will have no choice but to be stingy with the results. So why not do for your muscles what will enable them to do what you'd like them to do for you?!

Recall Psalm 38:10 at the start of this chapter: "My heart throbs, my strength fails me." After you've gradually built up your capacities for peak physical exertion, the intensity you generate on your strength-training exercises will literally have your "heart throbbing" until (or very close to the time) your "strength fails" you at the termination of a particular set of a given exercise, and I hope you'll find the process rather exhilarating!

And let's hark back for a second to Epictetus's advice and to our decathlon metaphor as well. There truly are different kinds of training required for long-distance running and for sprinting, and for the pentathlon as a whole. Some events rely more on strength and others on endurance. The fundamental differences in the proper training involve both *intensity* and *duration*. Keep this thought in mind, as we unpack its implications in the chapter ahead.

MUSCLE MASTERY TIPS AND FACTS #4

The Power of Negative Thinking
No, I'm not telling you to be a pessimist. I'm simply encouraging you to think more about the negative portion of each strength-training repetition. Without getting into advanced "negative only" training techniques, there are some simple ways you can emphasize the negative:

+ Go slow on the negative portion of each repetition. Traditional HIT methods recommend about four seconds. I often perform the *very last repetition* of my set much more slowly, lowering the weight nearly as slowly as possible.

+ On some exercises with a single movement arm, such as many leg-curl or bicep-curl machines, try this: using about 70 percent of the weight you'd normally use, raise the weight with *both* limbs, then gently shift the weight to *only one* as you lower it slowly. Alternate limbs through your normal set of repetitions.

+ Negatives can also be used when you lack the strength to perform positives. If you have difficulty performing chin-ups, for example, why not step onto a box or stool, start at the top of the movement, and simply lower yourself slowly? When you reach bottom, step up again and repeat. Over time, you may develop the strength to perform the positives as well.

Do negatives sparingly — and not to failure — and be extra careful to use proper form and natural breathing.

Chapter 5

Duration in Moderation

"He has appointed a time for
every matter and for every work."
Ecclesiastes 3:17

"Now, there are short and simple exercises which tire
the body rapidly, and so save time; and time is
something of which we ought to keep strict account."
Seneca

Almost two thousand years ago, the Roman philosopher Seneca knew some things about exercise (and the importance of time) that many modern fitness experts just can't seem to fathom today. (Of course, old Seneca wasn't constantly bombarded with infomercials about the latest fitness gadgets, machines, and routines.) What kinds of exercises was Seneca talking about? "Running, brandishing weights, and jumping" — in other words, demanding exercises that call forth brief and intense bursts of effort.

Intensity and *duration of effort*, you see, *are inversely proportional.* How's that? A well-known saying in HIT circles is that "you can train hard, or you can train long, but you can't do both." The more demanding the exercise, the shorter the time you're able to sustain it. The harder you work, the sooner you must stop. We all know this from experience. And the kind of exercise that maximizes physical strength is not only intense but also *brief.* Perhaps you've heard the saying, "Work smarter, not harder." Well, in the world of high-intensity strength training, working harder *is* smarter! Let's see why.

Aerobic and Anaerobic Exercise

The relationship between intensity and duration brings to mind one of the most fundamental distinctions in the field of exercise science — namely, the difference between *aerobic* and *anaerobic* exercise. Remember Epictetus's distinction in the last chapter between the different kinds of training required by the long-distance runner and the sprinter? He hit the nail on the head, millennia before the advent of formal exercise science. He understood the important difference between aerobic and anaerobic exercise. He just lacked our modern terminology.

Aerobic derives from the Greek words for "air" and for "life." Aerobic exercises are those done at a low enough intensity that the muscles can be supplied with oxygen as they continue to perform; walking, jogging, and bicycling are some examples. They demand more oxygen than our normal daily activities, so they kick our hearts and lungs into a higher gear. The lungs' role is obvious. We can hear and feel them work by our heavy breathing. The heart plays its role by more vigorously circulating the blood, which carries oxygen to our muscles.

Aerobic exercise is important because it builds the capacities of our cardiovascular and respiratory systems. *But aerobic exercise doesn't build much muscle.* This is where the big guns of anaerobic exercise are called in. Anaerobic exercise is done "without oxygen." It refers to exercise so intense that the body is not able to keep up with the muscles' demands, so a different kind of energy source is required. You don't need a deep understanding of the underlying biochemical processes to benefit from anaerobic training, so I'll just mention in passing that the energy for intense, anaerobic exercise comes primarily from glycogen, a precursor of blood sugar utilized by the muscles.

So, in a nutshell, *aerobic* refers to steady-state exercise that increases the demands on the hearts and lungs, but only at a level that can be maintained for a relatively long time — several minutes for most of us, to several hours for the highly trained endurance athlete such as a marathoner or a triathlete. *Anaerobic* refers to very intense activity that places much greater demands on the heart, lungs, and skeletal muscles, and which can be maintained for only a very brief time, from a few seconds up to about two minutes. *It is anaerobic exercise that makes us strong and makes our muscles grow.*

Back again to Epictetus's example. The long-distance runner performs moderately intense, long-lasting aerobic exercise. The sprinter performs extremely intense and brief anaerobic exercise. Take a look at the leg muscles of a top-notch marathon runner and compare them with the leg muscles of a top-notch sprinter. The sprinter, the athlete who performs intense, anaerobic exercise, will have much larger quadriceps, gluteus, hamstrings, and calves, since these are the engines that generate the power and speed the sprinter needs — engines built and fueled by high-intensity, anaerobic exercise.

Too many weight trainers make the mistake of performing their strength training like the marathon runner, rather than like the sprinter, and they end up with muscles to match. Strength training is anaerobic training. It must be intense and, therefore, of brief duration.

So how brief is brief? I'll fill in the details and show you the math in the chapters ahead, but note for now that a properly conducted set of a strength-building exercise will take approximately forty-eight to seventy-two seconds to complete. Thus, strength-training workouts covering the major muscles of the entire body can take as little as twenty minutes, including the rest periods between the exercises.

But Who Needs Strong Muscles?

We all do. Strong muscles are not just for bodybuilders, weight-lifters, football players, wrestlers, or baseball players (these days). Indeed, most people could not develop truly enormous muscles, no matter how hard they tried. But building our own muscles to reach their genetic potentials has practical advantages for everyone. For example:

• *Muscle cells burn more calories at rest than do fat cells*, thus enabling us to take in more calories without becoming fatter.

• *Increased bodily strength can help safeguard the heart from overexertion.* Tasks such as moving gardening rocks or mulch or furniture, or shoveling snow, may prove hazardous to the individual with weak muscles by producing dangerous demands on the heart. The same tasks may barely cause the strong individual to break a sweat.

• *The same kinds of brief, intense anaerobic exercise that strengthens our muscles also helps thicken our bones* to protect us from the ravages of osteoporosis and unwanted fractures later in life.

• *Developed muscles enhance the body's natural beauty.* (Ever take a peek at Michelangelo's Adam in the famous Creation scene adorning the dome of the Vatican?) Developed (not *over*-developed) muscles enhance the female form as well. We all need some fat, but it basically just sits there, shapelessly. It is our muscles that produce the natural and pleasing shapes and curves of our torsos and limbs.

• *Bodily strength serves as a foundation for charitable works.* When our muscles and bones are strong and we're brimming with energy, we're able to do more for our neighbor — especially those works that require physical exertion, whether shoveling your mom's driveway, moving furniture for the little old lady next door, helping your sister-in-law move (again), building a house for the needy, or whatever the case may be.

The Relationship Between
Muscular Strength and Endurance

Please allow me to elaborate a bit on an important point. Whereas longer, less-intense forms of training that focus on endurance (such as running) do little to enhance muscular strength, intense exercises that make your skeletal muscles stronger *also make them more enduring.* You'll find that as your muscles become capable of lifting greater loads for a given number of repetitions, you'll be able to perform *more* repetitions with a lighter load.

What's that got to do with the price of beans, you ask? Well, you may never be called on in daily life to lift some humungous stack of weights, but the strength that you develop in the gym can give you increased endurance to keep on ticking at sub-maximal, but still-demanding everyday tasks: from stacking boxes in your garage, to twisting a wrench or ratchet hundreds of times, to carrying bags of mulch to the backyard or groceries up the stairs, to giving your not-so-little-anymore kids an airplane spin. And while you're performing these works, your strong and enduring skeletal muscles will put lesser demands on your heart, joints, and back. So remember: endurance doesn't increase strength, but strength most definitely increases endurance.

Build a Temple, Not a Pyramid

Oh, one last thing with regard to this chapter's topic of brief workout duration. You do not have to perform multiple sets of exercises, at various numbers of repetitions, to become both stronger and more enduring. Thus, I don't endorse the common practice of "pyramiding" — beginning a workout with lighter weights and more repetitions, then progressing to heavier weights and fewer reps — that's a whole lot of sets, and it's the antithesis of brief, high-intensity strength training. Instead, I'll be advising you to do only *one* set per exercise. If you build your muscular strength with brief, intense workouts, muscular endurance will take care of itself. If you become strong at *any* repetition range within that "pyramid," you'll be strong in *all* of them. (Sneak preview — There is a similar direct relationship between muscular strength and explosive *speed*. Stay tuned for the next chapter's Muscle Mastery Tips and Facts box.)

Strength Endures

So there is duration, in brief. How fortuitous for us that the best form of strength training is also the briefest, leaving us time and energy for the other important activities in life. Seneca is right, and so is Ecclesiastes. Time is something of which we should keep "strict account," and there truly is a time for everything under the sun. We can all thank God that so little time is required for strength training.

Still, it is not yet time to rest. (That's what chapter 7 is for.) We've established that a given set of a strength-building exercise, and even an entire strength-building workout, will demand little time. But that still leaves open the question of *how often* we must perform these brief, intense sets of a given exercise, and *how often* we must perform entire strength workouts. Onward we go, then, to address the principal principle of *frequency*.

MUSCLE MASTERY TIPS AND FACTS #5

Muscle Fiber Recruitment

Skeletal muscle fibers operate on an all-or-none principle. Your body activates only the number of fibers needed to lift a given weight, but those fibers contract completely. The heavier the weight you lift, or the more your fatigue mounts with each repetition, the more muscle fibers will be called into play. This is another advantage of training in a high-intensity (HIT) fashion. You recruit the greatest number of muscle fibers in each of your sets, allowing very few fibers to loll about idly while the rest are getting down to business!

Chapter 6

Frequency for Results You'll See

"For everything there is a season,
and a time for every matter under heaven."
Ecclesiastes 3:1

"I confess that we all have an inborn affection
for our body; I confess that we are entrusted with
its guardianship. I do not maintain that the body
is not to be indulged at all; but I maintain that
we must not be slaves to it."
Seneca

The man's huge, fleshy, vein-laced calves underpinning dense and chiseled thighs stand out in bold relief as his feet dig into the earth for leverage. Shoulder muscles quiver and sweat beads on his brow as he leans into the rock, seeking the nooks and crannies to lock into with vise-like fingers. His eyes display a fierce determination, but also a profound weariness. A sigh of resignation and determination escapes his barrel chest, and he once more begins the boulder's slow ascent up the mountainside, creeping inch by inch before the grim, grizzled figure propelling it.

Have you ever heard of a Sisyphean task? Well, I just described its namesake. The ancient Greeks told of a mythical King of Corinth named Sisyphus. The ancient tale holds that Sisyphus was punished by Zeus by being fated to push a giant boulder up a hill, only to have it roll back down again every time it reached the top, forcing him to repeat the fruitless task for eternity.

Performing the same arduous physical tasks over and over again with no results to show for them is surely something we'll hope to avoid in our training pursuits! But there's another reason I introduce Sisyphus's tale in our chapter on frequency. If Sisyphus were a real man and his were a real task, poor Sisyphus would not be pushing that rock up that hill for very long. He'd soon become not only exhausted but debilitated. You see, undertaking maximal efforts too often can actually make us *weaker*. Thus, the *frequency* with which we conduct strenuous physical efforts is of paramount importance.

In this chapter, we'll address two key questions pertaining to the principle of frequency: 1) How often should we perform a set of a particular exercise within the same strength-training workout? and 2) How often should we work out?

The answers to these questions are not at all arbitrary. They flow logically from their interconnection to the principles of *progression*, *intensity*, and *duration* that we've addressed thus far, and the principles of *rest*, *form*, and *order* to come in the chapters ahead.

Times for Work, Times for Rest

During the sacrament of the Eucharist, how many times does the priest recite the words of consecration? The answer, of course, is *once*. Once the change in substance has been effected, there's no sensible reason for doing it again. During a workout, how many times need we repeat a properly performed set of a given exercise? The answer also happens to be *once*. Once the muscles have been worked to failure, or near-failure, there is no need to repeat the motion.

The Church tells us that the minimal frequency for attendance at Mass is *once per week*, based largely, of course, on God's third commandment, to keep holy the Lord's Day. What is the minimum frequency I'll recommend for strength training? It's also *once per week*. This isn't to say that benefit cannot be derived from more — in both cases, of course. The spiritual benefit of more frequent Mass attendance should be fairly obvious. But there's a physical lesson for us too. As, from one daily Mass to the next, there are different readings, psalms, prayers for specific feasts, and so on, when strength training is to be performed more than once weekly, the workouts can be varied in content and alternated to prevent overtraining.

In the very structure of the earth in its relationship to the universe, with its seasons and recurring cyclical patterns, God has built in times for everything under the sun. We need not repeat the same things every day. We are made to work and rest in alternation, and our physical and spiritual progress will best thrive when the frequency of our efforts is aligned with the capacities and rhythms of our human nature.

Pull the Trigger Only Once

Now, let's get down to some nitty-gritty strength-training business. We live in a culture where "more is better," and traditional methods of strength training apply this misguided concept within the gym. If one set of an exercise is good, many reason, then two must be better, right? (Get really advanced, I suppose, and soon you'll be ready for three, or four, or five, or . . . how many more?) Traditional training systems are thus based on *volume* of exercise, rather than on *intensity:* usually recommending three sets of a given exercise to beginners, and advancing from there, until you're ready to rent a space and live in the gym.

Let's recall the concepts of *intensity* and *duration*. Exercise must be intense to trigger muscle growth. That's what anaerobic exercise is all about. But intensity and duration are inversely proportional: you can work out hard or long, but not both. People who perform multiple sets of the same exercise are not giving their all on every set. They typically hold back a little, saving their maximum performance for the very last one. Of course, by the time they get there, they may have little strength left, or may still hold back for psychological reasons, daunted by the knowledge that multiple sets of many other exercises are still lurking in their immediate future. HIT training eliminates all the preliminaries, leaving only that very last (that is, the only) set.

Extra sets are not only unnecessary, but they can also be counterproductive, because they tap into the body's limited capacities to recover and rebuild from the cellular breakdown that occurs during strength-training sessions. Traditional strength-training sessions using the volume approach may take two hours just to train a couple of body parts. Compare this with the HIT approach, in which the entire body (thighs, calves, chest, back, shoulders, arms, abdominals) can be trained in as little as twenty minutes, because only one intense set is done for each exercise.

The volume approach confuses the principles of aerobic and anaerobic exercise. It makes strength training the equivalent of long-distance running, and not of sprinting, as should be the case. Do you remember how my workout partner and I like to say that "a little bit of something is better than a whole lot of nothing"? We consider multi-set volume training to be of low intensity, highly inefficient, and quite wasteful of one's precious time and energy. It typically includes "a whole lot of nothing."

Now, from decades of experience, I know quite well that some seasoned weight trainers will become almost hostile at the suggestion that one set is all that's needed. Experienced lifters are keenly aware of the dues they have paid for their muscles, in sweat and toil. Some think that by its brevity, the HIT approach makes false promises of an easy shortcut to size and strength. Unfortunately, they confuse working out *longer* with working out *harder*. They fail to grasp the crucial difference in *intensity of effort* between one set performed in HIT fashion and several performed in the traditional high-volume approach. A few may have also tried the HIT system and found it too demanding and uncomfortable for their liking. Finally, many people simply enjoy the experience and camaraderie of a long and leisurely workout (or aren't sure what else to do with their time).

Of course, many people who train according to traditional, high-volume methods, if blessed with the right genetics, actually do obtain large and strong muscles. During the typical high-volume workout, some sets *are* done with sufficient intensity to generate muscle growth. So, there is at least "a little bit of something" involved. But at what cost in wasted time and energy? And how many people with lesser genetics or fuller lives to live give up the quest, seeing no profit from such a huge investment of time and sweat?

The HIT philosophy maintains that one properly performed set of high-intensity exercise is sufficient to stimulate muscle growth. How can this be proven? The proof is in the pudding, and the main ingredient of this tasty pudding is our very first strength-building principle — *progression*. If you can perform only one intense set of an exercise and come back the next workout *stronger* than the workout before, then you have stimulated growth. You have progressed. In fact, if you carefully apply HIT methods, you should show improvements in strength on a regular basis, nearly every workout, until you near the limits of your God-given genetic potential.

Think of a high-intensity set of exercise as literally "triggering" a muscle's growth. If you pull a rifle's trigger and a bullet is released, what good does it do to continue pulling the trigger if the chamber has already been emptied? Our answer, then, to question 1 (How often should we perform a set of a particular exercise within the same strength-training workout?) is the best possible answer — the answer to our prayers. *Only one set is required for each strength-training exercise.*

How Many Workouts per Week?

Traditional strength-training methods do recognize, to some degree, the importance of rest and recuperation (we'll talk about it more in the next chapter). Typically, lifters are advised not to train their muscles two days in a row, but they're still recommended to work each muscle two to three times per week. Even in the first decades of the development of HIT methods, this was the standard recommendation. Why? Largely because it was believed that muscles would start to atrophy or shrink, losing size and strength, after three or four days.

But this belief has been found to be unfounded! Most seasoned lifters who lived and breathed by the traditional low-intensity, high-volume, and high-frequency methods of strength training (as I did in my teens during the 1970s) have noticed that after a layoff — for example, after a minor illness or a vacation, or when a demanding schedule forces us away from the gym for a week or even two — we often came back *stronger* than before. How could that be, if muscles start to fade away after just a few days?

Arthur Jones himself, the ingenious inventor of the Nautilus and MedX lines of strength-training and rehabilitation equipment (and, in my opinion, the father of HIT and Rational Strength Training), used to recommend three weekly training sessions, but later came to see that even less frequent training, along the lines of *one weekly session*, produced better results. Fortunately, I've noticed a recent positive trend in this regard, even among volume trainers. It's becoming more widely recognized that individual muscles need be trained only once per week for maximum size and strength.

Now, this may be done in only one weekly session involving the whole body, or in two to four briefer sessions in which different parts of the body are trained. Later, when we start to put together your own routine, we'll see which approach is best for you. For now, let's just remember the good news: that all we really need for productive strength training is *one weekly session*.

Seneca is on target once more. We want to become the masters, not the slaves, of our bodies. Thankfully, God has designed our muscles in such a way that it does take hard work, but just a little, to perfect them. At this point, do you feel due for a rest? Good, that's just where we're headed.

MUSCLE MASTERY TIPS AND FACTS #6

It's a Turtle . . . It's a Snail . . . It's Super Slow!
Here's another popular variation of HIT strength training that's worth trying for a "change of pace." Traditional HIT methods recognize that if repetitions are performed too quickly, momentum robs muscles of their work. That's why you should ordinarily shoot for roughly two-second positives and four-second negatives. But from time to time, you can try something that stops momentum in its tracks, such as Ken Hutchinson's "Super Slow Training." Here's how to do it: Use about 70 percent of the weight you'd use in a normal set. Starting very slowly and deliberately, take a full *ten* seconds to complete the positive. Lower the weight in four seconds, as usual, and start your second repetition. At about fourteen seconds per repetition, roughly four to six repetitions should get the job done.

Chapter 7

Rest to Grow Best

*"For whoever enters God's rest also ceases
from his labors as God did from his."*
Hebrews 4:9

*"The workout, understand, doesn't produce
muscle growth, but merely serves to stimulate the
body's growth mechanism into motion. It is the
body that produces the growth, but only if left
undisturbed during a sufficient rest period."*
Mike Mentzer

The book of Genesis tells us that on the seventh day of creation, God rested — even though He didn't *need* it, strictly speaking. In the seventh chapter of this book, we very appropriately come to the subject of *rest*.

If you'll recall from the previous chapter, for optimal strength training, we need to work out only once per week, and rest on the other six days! Let's examine why.

It was the late Mike Mentzer, a Mr. Universe and the proponent of his own "Heavy Duty" version of HIT strength training, who most forcefully argued for the true value of rest in a strength-training regimen. For him, when it comes to achieving muscular strength and size, strength training and rest share an equal value. *In other words, rest is every bit as important as exercise.*

This is because strength training stimulates muscle growth by causing minor cellular damage. The body, when allowed to rest and recuperate, then produces the growth to defend itself from a future assault of such magnitude. It devotes a portion of its resources to making those muscles bigger, stronger, and less vulnerable to damage. This adaptive process has been called *overcompensation* or *supercompensation*.

See how this interplay also ties in to the process of progression? Once the body has used the rest period to grow back stronger than before, it will take a slightly more intense and demanding stimulus the next workout to trigger the need for even more growth.

Bear Your Cross, Then Rest

In a sense, the muscle must suffer and go through a kind of "death" in order to come back to an even stronger "life." This is directly comparable to the paradox of the spiritual life, which is the paradox of the cross: we must die to ourselves in order to be reborn. As Jesus told us, "Truly, truly, I say to you, unless a grain of wheat falls into the earth and dies, it remains alone; but if it dies, it bears much fruit."[15] Jesus Himself, of course, demonstrated this most fully, and if we live for him, we can hope to have a share in his death, Resurrection, and glorified body.

In like fashion, the moral life involves a daily dying to self and a gradual strengthening of Christ-like habits. To cultivate the moral virtues, we have to "break down" our appetites: for physical pleasures, for venting of our anger and frustrations, for flaunting our talents and accomplishments. When we chastise our petty wills (usually a hard and uncomfortable task), we emerge bigger-hearted, stronger in goodness, and capable of greater feats of virtue and charity.

Recall, too, that Jesus told us, "If any man would come after me, let him deny himself and take up his cross daily and follow me."[16] For some people, a strength workout may indeed seem like a cross to bear. And even for those of us who truly enjoy it, there is no denying that some pain and discomfort accompany the kind of intense effort that is required to stimulate new growth. So, here is a direct physical-spiritual connection: suffering can be meritorious. Indeed, there's no reason we can't "offer up" to God the pain of our workouts, for the sake of truly suffering souls! (Years ago, when I'd run, I'd sometimes imagine that the discomfort came

[15] John 12:24.
[16] Luke 9:23.

from the agony of fat cells being burned up! Offering up the pain of our workouts for those in the spiritual fires of purgatory is a much more efficacious alternative!)

Further, offering up the pain of intense exercise is a more health-ful alternative to ascetic physical practices of bodily chastisement that could cause the body actual harm. True, not many Christians these days practice self-flagellation for its own sake, but I see no reason why similar benefit can't be obtained from the pain and sacrifice of making regular trips to the gym, if we expressly will it. A weight bench can be an excellent location for recollection and prayer.

Pain and fatigue were not part of God's original plan for the body (and they won't be in eternity), but they are our lot in this fallen world, and if we are to reap the benefits of strenuous train-ing, we must accordingly give our bodies regular periods of rest. It was after all, the same Jesus who called us to take up our crosses who also told us, "Come to me all who labor and are heavy laden, and I will give you rest."[17]

Man the Ramparts for Rampant Muscle Growth

This, then, is how muscles grow bigger and stronger: through alternating episodes of assault and defense. The weights batter down the muscles' ramparts. When the siege is lifted, the body re-sponds by rebuilding those ramparts a little bit higher and a little bit sturdier. It's a delicate process, because it's possible to batter those ramparts *too* thoroughly, to assault those muscles with *too* much strength training. *Overtraining*, typically in the form of too many sets, too many exercises, or too-frequent training sessions, can overrun the body's capacity to rebuild, leading to loss of

[17] Matt. 11:28.

strength, systemic illness, or damage to the muscles, tendons, ligaments, or joints. See how this dovetails with the principles of our previous chapters? Strength training should be done briefly and infrequently, to allow the body time for rest and recuperation.

Ramparts, by the way, call forts to my mind. The word *fort*, of course, is also related to the virtue of fortitude. Both derive from *fortis*, Latin for "strength." We build the virtue of fortitude in ourselves by mastering challenges, but we should seek challenges that will *tax*, not overwhelm, our current levels of strength. To do this, we need to temper our strength with humility and acquire the wisdom to know our limitations. Fortitude is our virtue, and cowardice, timidity, giving up, and not trying are its vices of deficiency. But there are vices of excess too — namely, temerity, foolhardiness, and recklessness; these mimic fortitude, but do not produce its virtuous results.

So, in our physical strength training, we must face down discomfort and discouragement with fortitude, but by that same virtue, we must avoid the follies of overtraining that can tear us down, rather than build us up. We must strive for that golden mean between exercise and rest. We will know we've achieved it by our results.

Two more key principles of strength training still await us as we fine-tune the knowledge of the fundamental principles of strength training that we'll put into practice later in the gym. So next let's consider *form*, and then a look at *order* will be in order.

MUSCLE MASTERY TIPS AND FACTS #7

The Relationship Between Strength and Size

It seems commonsensical that a bigger muscle is a stronger muscle, because muscles are the engines of our strength. Yet there are few professional bodybuilders in those "World's Strongest Man" competitions these days. In fact, there are some championship-level weightlifters with surprisingly little visible muscularity.

There are many factors besides muscle mass that contribute to a person's strength, such as skeletal proportions (which affect leverage) and neuromuscular factors. Some people, thanks to their genetics, have fantastic leverage, and can call in a tremendous number of their muscle fibers at any one time. They might be very strong without looking the part. Others with bigger muscles but less advantageous genetics might not be able to match the first group in strength. Most of us lie somewhere in the middle in our strength and size potentials.

Some people take the anomalies they have observed as proof that training for muscle size and muscle strength are two very different things. They conclude that by "pumping" their muscles with blood during multiple low-intensity sets (which produces a momentary size increase due to vascular congestion), they're giving them the best stimulation for growth. But that's not the case. The truth is, regardless of how your strength compares with that of others, *to make your muscles bigger, you must make them stronger.*

Chapter 8

Form Must Be the Norm

"The earth was without form, and void and darkness was upon the face of the deep, and the Spirit of God was moving on the face of the water."

Genesis 1:2

"The upper body is bent forward, taking the weight of the left leg, which must be thrown upward and go along with his right side . . . He turns his head to the far right and bends his body so as to see his ribs and to throw upward as if drawing water and throwing with his whole right side."

Philostratos

Have you seen a picture of the famous statue by the ancient Greek sculptor Myron called *The Discus Thrower*? Can you recall the perfectly proportioned physique, the placid facial expression, body twisted at the waist with discus held high, cocked and ready to be hurled? If so, maybe now the quotation from Philostratos at the beginning of this chapter will make sense to you, since in it he was describing that very statue. But why am I describing his description? Good question.

We've all heard the saying, "Anything worth doing is worth doing right." Who can argue with that? Well, in any kind of athletic endeavor, execution of correct *form* is essential to "doing it right." Proper posture and proper execution of bodily movements are required to maximize physical performance, but not *only* physical performance. Calling to mind again our hylomorphic human nature of intertwined body and soul, I'm sure you'll agree from personal experience that our physical postures also influence our *mental* operations and our *spiritual* attitudes.

Consider the bodily postures associated with formal prayer and liturgy: from the Sign of the Cross, to folded hands, to genuflection, to the planned alternations of sitting, kneeling, and standing. And those postures and gestures have their own proper form as well. (Picture a kind but stern old nun taking a grade-schooler to task for a sloppy, hasty Sign of the Cross; *she* knows that bodily forms can affect the mind and soul.) Even in our acts of private and public worship, our bodily postures serve the purposes of showing respect for God and of instilling in us a mental set of reverence and meditation. They focus our attention, still our irrelevant bodily motions, and prepare us for important spiritual business. When they have become habitual through regular practice, those very bodily motions will begin to trigger the proper spiritual response.

So, too, does form serve a very important purpose in our strength-training exercises. Without correct form, or the *manner of exercise performance*, strength training can be unproductive or, worse, lead to bad — and even dangerous — habits.

It's simply impossible to give our muscles a high-intensity stimulus if our exercises are not performed in the proper manner, *and yet*, form is often the most neglected aspect of strength training. Believe me, from my several decades of working in and working out in several gyms, I can tell you that proper exercise form, although *not* difficult to do, is quite rarely seen, because it is so seldom taught and understood.

Poor exercise form is most commonly exhibited by:
- partial range of motion;
- excessive speed of movement;
- improper body positioning.

Chances are our nun corrected her young student on these same three points. In like fashion (without scolding, though!), allow me to explain to you the three principles of proper form.

Full Range of Motion: No Cheating!

Perhaps the most common mistake in exercise performance is the failure to work through a muscle's entire range of motion. Remember that in order to stimulate muscles to grow, we must work them intensely within a set, thus calling into play the largest possible number of muscle fibers. To recruit the greatest number of muscle fibers, we must make the most of every exercise by moving through the greatest range of movement possible for the given exercise.

For an example, let's take a simple pressing movement such as the barbell bench press. This exercise has a pretty simply defined range of movement. You're lying on your back. The bar can go no lower than the point at which it rests on your chest, at about sternum level. The bar can go no higher than the point at which your arms are fully extended and your elbows are locked. So, there you have it. Just move the bar from a position resting on your chest until your arms are completely extended. Lower, repeat the complete motion until failure or near-failure, and your pectoral, front deltoid, and triceps muscles will thank you for it by growing a little bit stronger next workout.

Easier said than done, however. The most common mistake people make, even on a simple bench press, which has a limited range of motion to begin with, is to reduce its range of motion even further — in order to be able to lift (and be seen lifting) more. For, in a "compound" exercise, such as the bench press, that uses several muscles at once and ends up in a locked-out position, you can handle much more weight near the *end* of the motion than at the start, down there on your chest. Just look around at the gym sometime. Many people "cheat" this exercise by failing to bring the bar all the way down to their chest. They can handle more weight that way initially, but they are robbing themselves of the full muscle stimulation of performing the complete motion.

Let's watch Bubba and Joe, two eighteen-year-old weightlifting buddies. Bubba benches 150 pounds for ten repetitions, bringing the bar only halfway down to his chest. He chortles a little bit when Joe has to reduce the weight to 120 pounds for his set of ten, but Joe performs the exercise through the full range of motion.

Bubba might relish his illusion of superior strength, but it won't last long. Joe's muscles are receiving greater stimulation, and he'll soon be using far more than 150 pounds for good full reps, and his muscles will show it.

But wait. Well-intentioned but poorly informed lads like Bubba tend to drift into other ways to cheat on their form (and to cheat themselves in the process). A second way also ties into range of motion. For a barbell-pressing exercise, the farther apart you place your hands on the bar, the less distance the bar will travel. The muscles receive less stimulation, but you're able to lift more in the short run. Guys like Bubba tend to be real wide grippers, with hands spread well beyond the shoulders.

It's easier to obtain full range of motion on properly constructed (and adjusted) strength-building machines, but even here, be it a press like a chest press, overhead press, or leg press, or a pulling or rowing or curling motion, many trainees will make the mistake of performing only half or partial motions, usually at the end of the range of motion. Again, this may create an illusion of greater strength, because more weight can be used in this manner, but it does not stimulate as much future growth.

There's another benefit to using a full range of motion. Some exercises start by placing the muscles in a mildly pre-stretched position, which can enhance your flexibility as well as your strength. (I saw this myth of the "inflexible," "muscle-bound" weightlifter exploded in the early 1980s, when a bodybuilder named Tom Platz, owner of the most massive and muscularly developed thighs and hamstrings in the world, sat on a table and touched his head to his knees, with his legs straight and knees locked, right before my very eyes! I've *never* been able to do that myself.)

All right, enough on range of motion for a while. Let's move on and look at the next trick up young Bubba's sleeves.

Speed of Motion: Easy There, Lightning

You'd better look fast if you want to catch Bubba's next set, because he's really going to be moving! Bubba has found that he can lift greater poundage through the course of a set if he moves *really* fast. And if he brings the bar all the way down to his chest, chances are he's there for some quick rebound action. Bouncing a barbell off your chest, or simply contracting your muscles as hard and fast as possible right from the start, will bring the forces of momentum into play, allowing you to move more weight. This will give the appearance of more strength, but in reality, fewer muscle fibers will be recruited and less actual muscle strength and growth will be stimulated.

From my days at my local YMCA's dungeon-of-a-basement weight room in the 1970s, I remember a young guy like Bubba who milked momentum on the bench press for all it was worth. In fact, he so forcefully bounced the bar off his chest that he had a perpetual open wound over his sternum. He would compensate for this injury by placing a padded cushion made for barbells around the center of the bar. This in turn helped him generate even more momentum, thus further reducing actual muscle stimulation. It *also* reduced range of motion. So he was left with a big sore on his not-so-big chest.[18]

What is the *proper* speed of movement, then? As I relate in one of our Muscle Mastery Tips, most authorities of the HIT school recommend taking about two seconds to raise the weight and about twice as long, or four seconds, to lower it, thus ensuring that

---

[18] Please bear in mind, I'm not relating stories like these to put anyone down. I have my own share of fitness follies, and we'll come across some of those in the pages ahead. But I share these "Bubba stories" to help you avoid making the same silly, and sometimes dangerous, mistakes.

momentum will have little chance to rob the muscles of their rightful labor.

Elsewhere in this book, we'll talk about some variations on the theme of repetition speed that employ slower repetitions and even holds or pauses. For now, let's move on to the last important area of form.

Body Positioning: Keep It Straight and Firm

Looks like young Bubba is bench-pressing again, and this time he's going for his record and pulling out all the stops. Notice that he's arching upward from the hips. His behind is actually in the air, no longer in contact with the surface of the bench. Note, too, how his arms extend unevenly, as he seesaws the weight upward, boldly defying gravity, inch by awkward inch. You guessed it — the last common affront to exercise form that I'll address involves unseemly bodily contortions — wiggling, squirming, writhing, or tilting during a repetition.

Although I don't endorse weightlifting competitions for everyone, the sport of power lifting undeniably promotes proper form. Folks like Bubba who do partial repetitions, bounce the weight, writhe and twist and use uneven arm extension might be surprised to find that in official bench-press competitions, the bar must be allowed to sit motionless on one's chest before a judge claps to signal the start of the lift. Further, if you raise your bottom from the bench or extend your arms unevenly, the lift is no good. These rules are not arbitrary, like a fault line in tennis; rather, they flow from the principles of good, safe body positioning. They are just as important to Mom's or Grandpa's strength-training regimens as they are to high-level competitive power lifting. Following them will maximize muscle development and minimize the risk of injury.

There are other elements to proper form, such as breathing naturally and not holding your breath. A good fitness trainer can help you learn these and all the proper body mechanics specific to a given exercise. This is usually more easily done with machines than with free weights (barbells and dumbbells). Further, many of the advanced strength-training machines (like the MedX line) you find in gyms today even come with detailed laminated cards attached that illustrate proper form.

Recall once more the book of Genesis. The world itself was all void and darkness after all, until God's Spirit gave it *form*. With that in mind, let's move now to the bottom of the order, the last strength-training principle on our list: that of order itself.

MUSCLE MASTERY TIPS AND FACTS #8

Free Weights Versus Machines
Some strength trainers still debate the virtues of free weights (barbells and dumbbells) versus strength-training machines (such as Nautilus, Hammer Strength, Kaiser, Life Circuit, et al.) as if one were forced to choose one way or the other. In truth, they are all helpful tools for building muscular strength. Free weights have some advantages in that a host of exercises can be performed with a few simple bars and barbell plates. They also require balance and work many supportive muscles during each exercise. They can be dangerous, however, and most free-weight exercises do not provide resistance through a muscle's full range of motion. I built most of my own strength from free weights. Now, in my mid-forties, I still lift very heavy weights, but I use mostly machines, because they're easier to use and more time-efficient (no loading and unloading), they tend to work muscles through a more complete range of motion, and they leave me less prone to minor injuries, even when I'm working exceedingly hard. I know many other former serious weightlifters who adapt to the aging processes by lifting lighter weights for higher repetitions, and accepting smaller, weaker muscles as an inevitable result of aging. I prefer to keep my workouts short, sweet, and as heavy as possible, using impeccable form and mostly machines.

Actually, even in my peak days of power-lifting competition, I used both, but sparingly. Free weight *versus* machines? Why the *either-or*? They can both get the job done.

Chapter 9

Order Makes Workouts Shorter

Ordo rationis: order of reason.
That which governs human life according to
the principle of reason.

Ordo sapientae: order of wisdom.
That basic principle which orders human life
according to reason and wisdom.

Ordo caritas: order of charity.
That which refers to and is governed by or
in accord with, the principle of charity.

In part II of this book, we have sought to assemble an *ordo rationis* specific to our strength-training endeavors. I've tried to show how there are logical reasons for high-intensity training principles, and that these principles prescribe an *order*: a specific structure or arrangement of parts of something designed to enhance the functioning of the whole. In later sections, I hope to move us into an *ordo sapientae* of sorts, as we seek *prudently* to craft your own comprehensive strength, endurance, and dietary regimens. And finally, in the concluding chapter, we'll see how all this fits within an *ordo caritas*, as we examine the theological virtues of faith, hope, and charity, the highest of which is . . . (you already know it).

There is yet another sense of the word *order* that denotes proper *sequence*. It is this specific aspect of order that will be our special concern now. In the last chapter on form, we recalled that "a job worth doing is worth doing right." For this chapter, let's dust off the familiar saying "first things first." Here we will consider the proper order for strength-training exercises: which ones to do first, second, third, and so on, and how they logically fit into the whole of total fitness. For working out in the proper order is essential to working out *efficiently*: both with regard to maximizing muscle growth and to minimizing time spent in the gym.

The King of Exercises!

The body functions as a whole, an interrelated unit in which each part plays its role (see 1 Corinthians 12 for St. Paul's discourse on this topic). When you're working your leg muscles, for example, your heart and your lungs also kick in to support your efforts. Further, the body's adaptive response to strength training is to some extent *generalized*. The body has a natural tendency to keep its parts in proportion; thus, each specific exercise produces an indirect *general* effect of stimulating overall bodily growth, and the greater the muscle mass involved, the greater the overall stimulation.

Since long before HIT theory arose, lifters have called the squat (a deep-knee bend with a barbell across the shoulders) the "king of exercises." Why? Because it stimulates so many large muscles at the same time — the gluteus maximus, the muscles of the thighs and hamstrings, the muscles of the lower back, and the calves, plus assorted other muscles that play a supportive role in keeping your posture aligned during this most demanding exercise. It has been widely recognized that it's very difficult to attain maximum size and strength *even in the upper body* without doing squats (or an alternative, such as heavy leg presses); such is the power of the indirect effect produced by working such large muscle masses at the same time.

This realization affects the order of our exercises, dictating that the most demanding exercises with the greatest indirect effect are the most important and should be done *earliest* in the workout, when we are fresher and stronger. Thus, the recommended sequence for a strength-training workout runs something like this:

1. Hips, glutes, and thighs
2. Chest or back
3. Shoulders
4. Arms
5. Abdominals and lower back
6. Calves

There's some room for leeway here, and I'll give many concrete examples of variations later, but the general principle is that we will start with the most demanding exercises taxing the larger muscle groups, and work our way down to the less demanding exercises targeting the smaller muscle groups.

Rounding Out the Royal Court

There's another very important reason for this arrangement, and to help you grasp it fully, I must briefly address the difference between compound and isolation exercises. *Compound* exercises work several muscles at the same time and involve the rotation of multiple joints. Earlier I mentioned the bench press as an example of a compound exercise: it's performed primarily to stimulate growth in the large pectoral muscles of the chest, but other muscles, primarily those of the anterior deltoid (front shoulder) and triceps (back of the arm) must also assist. Movement occurs both around the shoulder and the elbow joints.

Other compound movements include overhead presses, and any kind of chin-up, pulldown, row, or leg-pressing motion. Most compound movements utilize the large muscle groups of the thighs, chest, and back. These are big, bad (you know I really mean good), demanding exercises. If you've been paying close attention, you might also suspect that these are the exercises that produce the greatest indirect effect, and you would be correct. Indeed, it is possible to construct very brief, yet reasonably thorough workouts using as little as three compound exercises to train the whole body.

But there's another issue, beyond the indirect effect. Those smaller muscles that assist in compound movements, such as the shoulders and triceps on pressing movements for the chest, or the biceps and forearm muscles for pulling movements for the upper back, also serve as weakest links. If those muscles are weakened, they may fail first, and you may reach failure on a chest press before your pectoral muscles have been adequately fatigued. Therefore, you should avoid (for one example) doing shoulder or triceps exercise *before* your major compound chest exercise.

In *isolation* exercises, the limbs or torso move around only one axis. For example, during a properly executed barbell curl, the arm bends only at the elbow. Whereas larger muscles can be trained with either compound exercises, isolation exercises, or both, many smaller muscles can be fully trained only with isolation exercises. Training the calves, for instance, requires some form of standing, bent over, or seated toe-raising motion with movement revolving only around the ankle joint.

Isolation exercises have their role to play, and later on, I'll detail how, but for this chapter on order, let's just remember these two key ideas: 1) we will start our workouts with the larger muscle groups and work our way down to the smaller ones, and 2) we will start with compound exercises and work our way to isolation exercises.

Now we have finished the fundamental principles of strength training (pretty simple, aren't they?). Next, we'll shift our focus from the *strength* of fortitude to the *endurance* of fortitude, and from the field of *anaerobic* exercise to the field of *aerobic* exercise. We'll switch from strengthening our skeletal muscles to strengthening our circulatory and respiratory systems, and from building muscle to burning fat. By the time we arrive at part V, we'll be ready to put *both* forms of training together in our quest for total fitness. Any questions at this point? I'm pretty sure there are, and that's why I'm going to keep on writing.

MUSCLE MASTERY TIPS AND FACTS #9

We're Just Warming Up

I haven't mentioned "warm-ups" yet. But I should now. It isn't a good idea to jump into a set of a strength-training exercise and exert full force while your muscles are "cold." Lifters traditionally "warm up" by doing one or more sets with lighter weights before moving on to their heavier sets. Sometimes, however, they expend so much energy on their warm-ups that their strength is half-spent by the time they reach their real sets. I recommend that you think about warm-up sets as you do your real sets, in terms of *doing the least amount necessary to get the job done safely*. Remember, if you perform a set in slow, controlled, high-intensity fashion, the first relatively easy repetitions at the start of your set serve as a built-in warm-up.

Here's what I do. My first exercise of the day is usually the leg press. Let's say I'm using 400 pounds for eight or ten repetitions. I will typically do about half that weight, 200 or so, for three slow and easy repetitions, just getting into the groove and getting myself physically and mentally prepared for the real set to follow. I then do not do warm-ups on the other leg exercises (if I do any others that day). Next, when starting my first upper-body exercise, usually a chest press, I'll follow a similar three-repetition warm-up with about 50 percent of my real weight. Then I rest a few seconds and get down to business. I do no other warm-ups for any other exercises — and sometimes I even skip the chest press warm-up.

Part III

Fortitude Endures:
Principles of Aerobic Training

"Now the principal act of fortitude is to endure."
St. Thomas Aquinas

Chapter 10

Heart, Soul, and Lungs: Formal Aerobic Exercise

"We should take walks outside so that the mind can be strengthened and refreshed by being outdoors as we breathe the fresh air."
Seneca

"Every athlete exercises self-control in all things. They do it to receive a perishable wreath, but we, an imperishable. Well, I do not run aimlessly, I do not box as one beating the air; but I pommel my body and subdue it, lest after preaching to others, I myself should be disqualified."
1 Corinthians 9:25-27

The virtue of fortitude is not just about feats of strength or dramatic and isolated acts of daring and bravery; it's also about staying the course, about enduring discomforts for longer periods. Fortitude in this sense is embodied by the less-intense, but longer-lasting efforts required by aerobic training: the second key component of developing total fitness.

Aerobic Capacity and Beneficial Effects

The body's capacity for aerobic (literally, "with air or oxygen") exercise can be seen in three key areas:[19]

• The capacity to breathe in large quantities of air.

• The capacity to circulate large volumes of blood throughout the body.

• The ability to deliver oxygen to all parts of the body.

Now, when we're talking about breathing and circulating, it's obvious that the lungs and the heart are involved in a big way. But they're not the only parts of the body that benefit. Nearly all of the body's systems can derive some benefit from aerobic exercise. Let's

[19] I borrow here in paraphrase from Dr. Kenneth Cooper's book *The New Aerobics*. Dr. Cooper could properly be called the "Father of Aerobics" due to the widespread and lasting influence of his book *Aerobics*, first published in 1968.

begin to examine them by looking next at four key *aerobic training effects:*

+ Strengthening of the muscles that are involved in respiration (breathing).

+ Increase of the heart's pumping capacity, delivering more blood to the lungs and other parts of the body with each stroke and allowing the heart to do its everyday job with less stress.

+ Improvement of muscle tone and general circulation. (Our skeletal muscles have been called "peripheral hearts" because their alternating bouts of contraction and relaxation help keep the blood pumping on its course throughout the body. Aerobic exercise makes them more efficient pumps as well.)

+ Increase both in the total amount of blood circulating in the body and in the oxygen-carrying components in the blood: namely, the red blood cells and the amount of oxygen-rich hemoglobin they carry.

So, we can see that aerobic conditioning benefits our hearts, lungs, diaphragms, and skeletal muscles, and even the chemical composition of our blood. But there's even more. Those who do aerobic exercise may also notice benefits to their *digestive* systems, both through improved circulation to the digestive organs and because the physical motion of exercise gives the body a mechanical boost in moving things along their natural course. The *skeletal* system can benefit from weight-bearing aerobic exercise, by stimulating and thickening the bones. Aerobic exercise can further help greatly in terms of *weight control*, both because of the calories burned during aerobic exercise and because an aerobically conditioned body may continue to burn calories at a higher rate for hours after an aerobic session has ended.

Aerobic exercise can also boast a host of positive *psychological* effects: the potential cognitive benefits of increased circulation to the brain, the release of pleasurable and mood-enhancing endorphins, a sense of relaxation and release from stress and tension — not to mention the sense of satisfaction in knowing that you're helping rid your body of unneeded fat accumulation!

Oh yes, and in this context, I must not forget to mention that aerobic exercise, and especially the normal daily activities I'll describe in the next chapter, can be easily integrated with *spiritual* exercises, such as prayer, meditation, or absorption in sacred music.

Aerobic Training Principles

Do you recall the seven basic principles of anaerobic strength training that we covered in part II? Here they are again: progression, intensity, duration, frequency, rest, form, and order. We could also think of aerobic training in these terms, but they must be adapted to this different form of training. Let's do this in brief.

Progression in aerobic exercise is measured not in repetitions performed or weight lifted, but in terms of increased speed and increased duration of exercise.

Intensity is very important, but aerobic exercise calls for a moderate, rather than a high level of intensity. Accordingly, the optimal intensity of aerobic exercise can be measured by a heart rate during exercise of approximately 65 to 85 percent of maximum heart rate.

Duration is also different, with the barest-bones-minimum time for aerobic exercise being about a twelve-minute session, with thirty minutes to an hour being preferable, depending on the particular exercise.

Frequency also differs here. Since aerobic exercise is of lower intensity, it can be repeated more frequently, with three weekly sessions being the usual minimum recommendation.

Rest is still important, but because aerobic exercise is less intense, less rest is needed between sessions (which is why we can work out more frequently).

Proper exercise *form* is as important in aerobic exercise as in anaerobic exercise, both to stimulate desired results and to avoid injury.

Finally, *order* also plays a part, but not in quite the same way. Anaerobic exercise typically involves a circuit of several different exercises, while aerobic training usually entails a longer bout of just one exercise. Order plays a bigger role in aerobic exercise with regard to the intensity. For example, we will see the importance of starting up easily in a warm-up, exercising more intensely for a while, and then easing off again at the end in a cool-down period. With a quick peek at some basic principles under our belts, let's take a closer look at some aerobic exercises that could actually help remove some of that fat from under those belts.

Major Aerobic Exercises

Walking is perhaps the simplest and most natural form of aerobic exercise. Just put on some good shoes, clothing suited to the weather, and head out your front door.

Walking is a great exercise for beginners, because it can be performed at very low levels of exertion simply by going slowly. Although this will vary according to the characteristics (such as bodyweight and metabolism) of each individual, you can estimate that walking burns about a hundred calories per mile. Bearing in mind that there are some 3,500 calories in a pound of fat, you would have to walk about thirty-five miles to get rid of a pound of the stuff. Yikes!

But wait a minute, Rome wasn't built in a day, and neither was that fat around our waistlines. If you were to walk two miles a day (eventually covered in thirty minutes or so) five days per week, that would burn about another 1,000 calories per week, yielding the loss of a pound every three and a half weeks or about fifteen pounds in a year, simply by walking and leaving your diet unchanged. If you also did the minimum recommended strength-training regimen you'd also burn a couple of hundred more calories per week, and add some muscle tissue that requires more calories at rest just to sustain it. Add these together with a modest improvement in diet, and your fat loss can be quite substantial.

Running or jogging is another potent and popular form of aerobic exercise. Because you move faster while running than while walking, you cover a greater distance and burn more calories in less time. It was also long believed that running and walking burned the same number of calories *per mile* (since you're carrying your body weight the same distance), but more recent studies indicate that running actually burns more calories per mile, as well as *per minute*, because of the greater energy exerted in the bounding motion of running that lifts the entire body off the ground.

In any event, running can be a very powerful and efficient form of aerobic exercise. I've seen from personal experience and from friends' anecdotal evidence that running also seems to trigger fat loss like nothing else. The body seems to defend itself in an adaptive response, as if to say, "If I'm gonna have to lug him around like this for miles on end, by gum, I'm gonna make sure there's less o' him I gotta lug!" (or something like that; your body may be more eloquent).

It's relatively easy to get our heart into the aerobic training "zone" in just a few minutes. As little as three twenty-minute runs per week can have a significant aerobic training effect. Of course, your age, bodyweight, and fitness level will determine how much ground you could cover in that time. Good aerobics books (I recommend those of Dr. Kenneth Cooper) will have charts to show you what you can expect, based on your own condition.

Bicycling complements running very well by exercising different muscles of the legs. Whereas running puts those calf and hamstring muscles to the test, you'll find that serious bicyclists have solid and muscular quadriceps. Further, bicycling is a low-impact exercise, meaning that your joints do not suffer the repetitive, jarring concussions that are an inevitable result of every step of every run. (Oops, I hope I haven't completely chased you away from running — remember, *moderation* is the thing. Further, those calf and thigh muscles we're building from strength training will serve as biological shock absorbers for our joints.)

Swimming is an excellent choice for those with an aquatic bent. Needless to say, it complements running and biking very well by working the muscles of the upper body as well as the lower. Further, there's almost no impact at all (unless you misjudge a turn and hit your head on the side of the pool).

You do *not* have to do all of these forms of aerobic exercise. Any one will suffice, but alternating two or more of them on different days can be very effective. It provides variety and gives some groups of muscles additional rest while others are called into play. Speaking of play, when you really get these activities down, there's no reason they can't be rather fun.

But remember, not even triathlon training will produce *total* physical fitness. Aerobic activities by themselves will go only a little way toward the production of muscular strength. A triathlete who doesn't also strength-train might be able to keep his body moving for hours on end, but he might not last two seconds trying to match the workout of a seasoned strength athlete. In most cases, he would lack the muscular strength to perform, with the same poundage, even the very first repetition of the very first exercise in a strength athlete's high-intensity workout. Many seasoned strength athletes can perform their sets of ten or more repetitions with weights far exceeding what pure endurance athletes can lift even once.

Strength and Endurance Combined?

I was once involved in a biathlon of sorts that actually combined strength and endurance activities. Called a "Pump-and-Run" competition, it involved performing bench presses with one's body weight (or a percentage thereof for older competitors) for as many repetitions as possible, and then completing a 5K (3.1-mile) running race. For every successful repetition on the bench press, fifteen seconds was shaved off our running time.

How'd I do? Well, this competition pre-dated my return to leanness (I'll tell you about it later on), so although I had the best bench-press performance, I had one of the worst running times.

Now, five years older but weighing thirty-five pounds less, without any loss in benching power, and running almost two minutes faster per mile, I would love to do this competition again, but alas, the "Pump-and-Run" pumped and ran, and I haven't seen it again in my area. I did have a nice consolation prize, however. The man who won the overall competition was a very slight, but strong runner over the age of fifty. Near the end of my run, he actually came back and ran along to bolster my fortitude to keep running hard to the very end. After the event, he told me that he had taken a weightlifting class from me at the YMCA in the mid-1970s. That was great. Although I wasn't the champion, I gladly settled for being the trainer of the champion!

Enough of the aerobic and anaerobic nostalgia! It's time to get back to business.

Although in a book of this size, I certainly couldn't, in *justice*, give aerobic training its full due, I think I must at least elaborate more at this point on the concept of intensity in aerobic training and provide a simple way to measure it.

Measuring Aerobic Intensity

If you'll recall, for anaerobic strength training, we defined *intensity* as "percentage of momentary muscular effort." We noted that it's very difficult to measure until you reach 100 percent intensity — where your muscles fail and you can't complete another full repetition. Further, we noted that it was a good thing to arrive at (or at least near) that event. HIT, after all, stands for *High*-Intensity Training.

In a sense, we might also describe aerobic intensity as "percentage of momentary muscular effort" — if the muscle we're referring to is the *heart*. Each of us has a natural maximum heart rate. Under extreme exertion, a healthy heart will beat faster and faster, until it tops out and can beat no faster, kind of like the maximum number of rpm that an engine can generate. This maximum rate varies with age, and pretty regularly, too — there are some individual differences here, but they are usually slight. A good rule of thumb for estimating your maximum heart rate is:

Maximum heart rate (beats per minute) = 220 - Your age

Now, depending upon your current level of fitness, aerobic activity is usually performed in the range of 65 to 85 percent of

estimated maximum heart rate. Here's a chart with rough estimates by age:

AGE	MAXIMUM HEART RATE	AEROBIC TRAINING RANGE
20	200	130-170
30	190	124-161
40	180	117-153
50	170	111-145
60	160	104-136
70	150	98-129

Bear in mind that the average adult male's resting heart rate is
about seventy-two beats per minute (eighty for women), give or
take a few beats based on individual genetic differences. For most
people, several months of aerobic training will tend to reduce the
resting heart rate by several beats per minute, as the heart becomes
a more efficient pump. Many computerized exercise machines
such as treadmills and exercise bicycles have electronic heart-rate
monitors built right in, to tell you how fast your ticker is ticking
while you're stepping or peddling away. That's just great. Some of
these machines also have an aerobic training range chart like the
one above, or a graph, labeled right there on the machine's control
panel as well. Bully, I say!

But not *essential*. The simplest and most important guideline to
follow is your own comfort level. If you feel as if you could go on
forever, you're probably not working hard enough. If you must stop
after just a few minutes, you've exceeded your aerobic capacity
and you're moving into anaerobic territory. Please save that for
strength training. You should strive for a perceived *moderate* level
of exertion. You may find that *your* optimal aerobic heart rate is a
bit higher or lower than the chart suggests. An often-cited rule of

thumb is to do aerobic exercise at such a pace that you would be able to carry on a conversation with another person, if you so desired. In other words, you should leave enough breath on reserve to allow you to talk as well as walk (or run or bike).

On Running the Good Race
(and Walking the Good Walk)

Let's reflect for a moment on our opening quotations from Seneca and St. Paul, since they both refer to an aerobic activity recommended in this chapter (walking for Seneca and running for St. Paul), but more important, because they serve to remind me of the need to make a very important point regarding a *Christian* approach to physical culture (a theology of body*building*, as I called it once before).

The Roman Stoic Seneca, we've seen, was quite an advocate of the credo *mens sana in corpore sano* ("a healthy mind in a healthy body"). Indeed, the Greeks and Romans are famous for their emphasis on the importance of perfecting both mind and body (and some philosophers were even known for walking while they taught). The wisest of the ancient Stoic philosophers, such as Seneca and the Greek Epictetus, also had much in their philosophies of ethics to commend them to early Christian thinkers. The Stoics strove to live lives of virtue and to follow God, as they conceived him. They condemned gladiatorial combat, argued for the humane treatment of slaves, argued in favor of women's equal capacity for intellectual and moral virtue, and proclaimed a universal brotherhood of men.

We give those classical Greeks and Romans due credit for their emphasis on a trained harmony of mind and body. But as Pope Pius XII stated so well, "In the field of physical culture, the Christian concept needs to receive nothing from the outside, but has much to give." The Christian conception of total fitness trumps even the noblest pagan's, because he ultimately perfects his body not just for himself, but for the greater glory of his Maker. And as the Christian's body grows in its prowess, in its physical capacity to endure, it becomes a more untiring servant of God and one's neighbor.

St. Paul drew on the metaphor of physical endurance when he famously compared the Christian life to running a race.[20] This is no surprise, considering that Paul grew up in Tarsus among ancient Greeks. He saw how Greek athletes were willing to work so hard and pommel their bodies, simply to win some fleeting fame and a laurel wreath. How much greater is that imperishable prize for which the athlete in Christ trains! St. Paul would have us train as spiritual athletes, not merely by walking, but by vigorously running and boxing for all we're worth, enduring all the while and staying the course to the very end, in order to do God's work and to become truly fit, *fit for eternal life*.

[20] 2 Tim. 4:7-8.

MUSCLE MASTERY TIPS AND FACTS #10

Cardiac Caveats

Did you read the tip about strength-training warm-ups in the last chapter? Now it's time to consider the warm-up for cardiovascular exercise, where it plays a more important role. It's neither healthy nor nice to demand that your heart suddenly go from rest to pumping like crazy. In aerobic exercise, it's best to take up to five minutes or so, gradually increasing the intensity of your activity as your heart rate gradually increases. Further, it's just as important to end with a few minutes of milder activity (such as a walk after a run) so that your heart rate may slowly return to normal. Abruptly ending intense aerobic exercise can have life-threatening implications for some people. So remember, start and end your workouts gently.

Chapter 11

Real Work Works:
The Value of Normal Daily Activities

"In all toil there is profit."
Proverbs 14:23

"Ora et labora: Pray and work."
Monastic Motto

"I began to look at household chores in a whole new light . . . I'd become a veritable white tornado — something between Mr. Universe and Mr. Clean — and my wife and neighbors much preferred me for it.
Bryant Stamford, Ph.D.

When I was a teen obsessed with the world of weightlifting, my father, a plasterer by trade, would frequently say to me, "Here, if you want to work out, I've got a *real* workout for you." It usually involved something like bringing him huge, heavy buckets of water or plaster, or contorting into some strange position to hold on to an auto part for several hours (seemingly) while he put it back on the car. (My brother and I never did grow fond of plastering or auto repair. Today we hire such things out!)

I'll admit that we did admire Dad's muscularity, though. His forearms in particular were like Popeye's — large, sinewy, hairy, and laced with thick veins from working with a heavy trowel full of plaster on the job, and with wrenches and pliers in his spare time. Still, I scoffed at the idea that helping him would in any way merit the title of a "workout." No, that lofty title was reserved to weight-room work only!

Today, I can appreciate Dad's wisdom on the value of old-fashioned labor, and I hope my own sons will be receptive to it. When it comes to being physically fit, strong, and enduring, *real work works!* It has its role to play, ideally *alongside* more formal strength and endurance training.

Let's consider, then, some ways that our own house, yard, or office building can function as a veritable gymnasium (without the membership fees). Further, I'll highlight how many of our normal daily physical activities can lend themselves to concomitant *spiritual* exercise as well.

Real Work Versus Aerobic Exercise?

I find it fascinating how various strength-training and aerobics fitness experts take such diverging views on just how (and even if) formal aerobic training should be performed. A few proponents of the HIT school have argued that formal aerobic exercise has been highly overrated. Ellington Darden argues, for example (and has some scientific research to back up his claim), that traditional steady-state aerobic exercises such as running or biking are unnecessary or even counterproductive. Why? Because it's possible to do high-intensity strength-training circuits with so little time between sets that your heart rate can stay in the aerobic training zone the whole time. Once you've completed such intense total strength and endurance training, additional endurance sessions could tap into your capacity to recover and grow between workouts.

This may be so, but believe me, it's a very demanding way to train, and most people will probably prefer to separate out their strength training from their cardiovascular endurance workouts. Having done both, my preference is definitely for separate aerobic training. Most fitness experts say the same, but there are some differences of opinion as to how it should be carried out. I think some of the differences boil down to the experts' (and their readers') personality types.

Take Kenneth Cooper's approach, for example. Open up one of his books, and you'll be amazed by the abundance of scientifically derived charts and tables. For precise individuals who like clear-cut goals and fine-tuned record-keeping, his books are where to go. Others, such as the late running guru and cardiologist George Sheehan, focus on the sensual and psychological experience of aerobic exercise, without worrying so much about all the scientific and record-keeping detail.

The Value of Normal Daily Activities

Fitness *Without* Exercise?

One of the most surprising perspectives on aerobic exercise that I've come across comes from Bryant Stamford, an exercise physiologist and former runner who argues that you really don't *have to* do formal aerobic exercise at all. This is pretty startling. After all, it's one thing for a weight-lifting musclehead to pooh-pooh aerobic exercise, but coming from a runner and exercise physiologist, that's a whole different ball game! What can we make of that?

Well, there might be something to it.

In the 1970s and 1980s, not long after the benefits of aerobic training within a target heart-rate zone became widely known, most fitness-minded folks came to regard the normal physical activities of daily life as something that just "didn't count" as real exercise. My eyes were opened to this error several years ago when I read the aforementioned book by Stamford, *Fitness Without Exercise*, which claimed that in recent decades, aerobics have been oversold as a panacea for our physical ills, leading us to foolishly ignore the value of good, old-fashioned normal daily activity.

Stamford and his co-author, Porter Shimer, point out that the classic studies showing the health benefits of moderate exercise have actually used data from normal physical activities such as walking and working, rather than from formal aerobic exercise studies. They also share some compelling personal anecdotes. Shimer, for instance, tells of a very aged but healthy neighbor who would smile at him from his garden next door while Shimer spent hours riding to nowhere on his exercise bike!

Stamford and Shimer do not rule out formal exercise entirely. Stamford admits to enjoying a weekly weightlifting workout with his sons, and Shimer still does aerobics, but in much smaller doses. But the clear take-home message is that formal aerobic exercise is not *essential*. After all, billions of human beings kept themselves lean and fit for ages before the discovery of the "aerobics revolution"!

I'll say it again: *You can lead a healthy life and be reasonably fit by eating sensibly and burning plenty of calories through a moderately active lifestyle.*

When I first made this discovery, I completely abandoned aerobic training for a while in favor of increased physical activities. The problem was, I really *enjoy* the exhilarating feeling that comes from aerobic workouts, especially after sitting in my office all day. Eventually I decided to *moderate, not eliminate* my desire for aerobic workouts. I can rest easier if I do aerobic training less often, or more briefly, knowing that I'm also burning calories and doing my body good if I'm just out mowing the lawn, washing the cars, or even vacuuming the carpets (and my wife stands behind me 100 percent!).

But, if you *don't* like aerobic exercise, or can't seem to justify the time for it, if you do your once-weekly strength workout, eat a sensible and moderate diet, and don't spend your regular daily life on the couch, you may consider the formal aerobic activities of the previous chapter as *optional*.

And speaking of options, here's one more. If you live in a climate with pretty well-defined seasons (such as the cold winters and hot summers here in central Illinois), your approach to integrating formal aerobic exercise with normal daily activities might well vary according to the seasons, such as pursuing more formal indoor aerobic activities in the winter months and relying more on outdoor normal daily activities when the weather is nicer. I do this to some extent, although I run more from May through September when it feels so exhilarating to breathe in the great outdoors, lungful by gasping lungful!

The Value of Normal Daily Activities

House Aerobics:
Calorie Burners That Get the Jobs Done

Before I catalog my suggestions for good, calorie-burning activities of daily life, note that although some fitness books provide estimates of calories burned per hour for many of the activities I'll list, I don't think that information is necessary. In fact, I don't recommend precisely tracking your calories that go in and out. Remember, one of our key themes is that attaining physical fitness has been needlessly overcomplicated. You'll know if you're doing enough by the results of your activities. Your scales, your tape measure, your mirror, even your blue jeans will tell you plainly enough.

Here we go. If you really want to get serious about these normal daily activities or "house aerobics," if you will, go set your kitchen timer for thirty minutes for your first "workout." Better yet, first turn on your stereo or your portable music player, and put in a CD or go to your MP3 player's music list. Select one of Anton Bruckner's Masses, or one of Beethoven's, or some Gregorian Chant, or other sacred music that perhaps includes Bruckner's or Schubert's *Ave Maria*, or better yet, something that strikes a spiritual chord with *you*. Next, take a deep breath, and without a warm-up, prepare to do one or more of the following exercises (in good form, of course, but in no particular order).

EXERCISES FOR YOUR TEMPLE (AND YOUR HOUSE)

1. *Washing and drying dishes* (or loading and unloading the dishwashing machine). You might even be on your way toward building your own Popeye-like forearms if the kids didn't soak their bowls of hot cereal or plates of spaghetti.

2. *Doing laundry*, including running around the house to gather the dirties, and/or folding the clean stuff and then running, walking, or bicycling around the house to put them away.

3. *Walking your dog.* (You'll also be helping him achieve Total Fitness for Dogs.)

4. *Vacuuming the carpets or sweeping the hardwood floors or tiles.* The pushing will work those pecs (chest muscles) a little bit and the pulling will give your lats (upper back muscles) a little something to think about between strength workouts.

5. *Grocery shopping.* You'll find that your cart becomes progressively heavier as you work your way through the aisles. (In the next two chapters, we'll talk a little bit about what to put into the cart.)

6. *Putting away the groceries* (I don't mean into your stomach!) when you get back home.

7. *Dusting* will burn a few calories and give your house a lemony-fresh scent as you perform other house-aerobic exercises.

8. *Window-washing,* inside and out, is a great way to work and stretch your arms, shoulders, and the oblique muscles on the sides of your waist.

9. *Lawn mowing* (preferably not while seated). Think of it as a high-intensity version of vacuuming.

10. *Picking up sticks.* (I guess I should have made this number 5 or 6.)

11. *Washing your car.* This is much like the outdoor version of window-washing and should actually include some window washing as well. (No drive-thru washes.)

12. *Stair-climbing at the office.* Your floor is too high for that? Can you get off the elevator just a couple of flights below your floor and hike the rest of the way? If so, you can hop off the elevator a floor or two lower as time goes by.

13. *Going down the stairs.* This is much easier on the legs and lungs, but still burns about 40 percent of the calories as climbing up the stairs, so it's nothing to sneeze at (unless your stairwell is very dusty).

14. If you're really feeling spunky, do a heavy-duty cleaning job on the garage, the basement, or a really big closet. This will provide plenty of bending, reaching, lifting, and so forth.

15. Gardening. Uproot some roses. Trim some weeds, but don't forget to smell them first. (Just checking to see whether you're still paying attention.)

16. Pumping irons (and ironing boards). If you're the type to go to the gym in the morning before work, burn a few calories in the evening by pressing out your work clothes the night before. Better yet, prepare a healthy lunch while you're at it, and tuck it in the refrigerator. Still need to burn more calories? Clean the refrigerator while you're at it! (Easy for me to say, huh?)

17. Dancing (with or without the stars). My wife and I signed up for dancing classes (ballroom, Latin, and even disco) right in the middle of the period of my fat loss last year. Although I still hope readers will never catch sight of me on a dance floor, I really think my dancing shoes helped my running shoes shed several pounds of my own ungraceful blubber!

Perhaps some skeptical readers are wondering at this point if I actually do all these things myself, especially the household chores. Well, you'll just have to ask my wife (but remember that *somebody* has to find time to sit, drink coffee, and write books). Seriously, though, these are mere suggestions, and I'm sure you can come up with more that are compatible with your own life routines.

The main point is to *change our perspective* on these little daily labors. They need not be drudgery. Some may burn but a few calories here or there, but add them all together, and their effects can really be substantial. We can use them to help us become fit, both physically and spiritually, if we put our bodies, minds, and souls into them.

The potential spiritual benefits of good old-fashioned work have been known for millennia, of course. *Ora et labora*, pray and work, is an ages-old monastic credo, a Christian call to the highest actions of the mind and body. St. Paul advised us to pray always.[21] There's no reason our minds can't be focused on higher things while carrying out those little daily activities that improve both our houses and our "temples," burn calories, and get jobs done. Just as we can "offer up" the discomfort of intense strength training, we can also "offer up" the toil of laborious chores — and profit in our hearts and waistlines in the meanwhile.

---

[21] 1 Thess. 5:17.

MUSCLE MASTERY TIPS AND FACTS #11

The Heat Is On

Here are a couple of nice little advantages that normal daily activities can claim over more formal and intense aerobic workouts. First, it isn't wise to attempt a demanding aerobic workout within about two hours of your last meal, when food is still in your stomach. The bigger the meal, the longer you may have to wait. Milder activities, however, such as getting up and doing those dishes, strolling with your spouse, or walking the dog, can be done without delay. Further, by performing those activities with food in your stomach, you may burn even more calories per minute, due to a physiological phenomenon known as the "thermic" or "thermogenic" (heat-generating) effect. After we eat a meal, the body's metabolic rate may increase by about 10 percent as digestion gets into gear, and by performing mild bodily activity during that time, calories may be burned at an even greater rate. So, consider "striking while the iron is hot" by getting up and moving about while your body's metabolic furnace has kicked in, within a half-hour to an hour after your last meal.

Part IV

Temperance:
Dietary Self-Mastery

"The end and rule of temperance itself is happiness."
St. Thomas Aquinas

Chapter 12

Habit, Not Diet

"Too much or too little gymnastic exercise is fatal to strength. Similarly, too much or too little meat and drink is fatal to health, whereas a suitable amount produces, increases, and sustains it."
Aristotle

"Beauty is a foremost attribute of temperance which above all hinders a man from being defiled."
St. Thomas Aquinas

Who would have thought that *temperance*, seemingly the dowdiest and least exciting of virtues, could be the key to happiness, strength, and beauty? It's true. But don't just take my word for it. Take another look at the last three quotations, from St. Thomas Aquinas and Aristotle. As we build bodily strength and beautify our physical forms, temperance allows us to control our appetites, guide them by the *golden mean*, and channel them toward the happiness that comes from making the most of our physical selves.

The *golden mean* of temperance is especially important to proper diet. There are no perfectly virtuous foods that can be eaten with total abandon. Neither are there purely evil foods that must be completely abandoned (although some *are* rather shady characters). Virtuous eating habits are to be understood rather in terms of *proper portion size* and *reasonable quantity of overall daily food intake*.

Diet? Don't Try It

Up to this point, we've looked at the proper principles and techniques for building our temples, both inside and out. Now it's time to look at the building materials: the foods we eat. What kind of materials should we use, and how much do we need?

Unfortunately, a quick look around us (or simply down toward our own middles) will reveal that most of us in this blessed nation use more building materials than necessary. Our bodies have gone from temples to overstock supply warehouses! We're pretty sure that we eat the wrong things, or eat too much, or both. And we don't take it lying down. No, we act on it in a big way. What do we do? Well, we buy diet books, that's what we do!

Diet books are a very successful literary genre (exceeded, perhaps, only by cookbooks). As I write, the number-one nonfiction bestseller on Amazon.com is indeed a diet book (perhaps it's the one-millionth diet book in print and readers are celebrating by buying it). But let's bear in mind what author Covert Bailey once wrote in, not a diet book, but in an exercise book (*Fit or Fat*): "The American public has been dieting for twenty-five years — and has gained five pounds." Well, that was written thirty years ago, and we've gained more than another five pounds.

What am I saying here? Exercise is everything and diet for naught? Not at all. To attain a healthy and pleasing leanness, we need *both*; and in fact, given a forced-choice scenario, I would say that diet is *more* important than exercise (in keeping low levels of body fat, that is, *not* in building strength and cardiovascular endurance). Then what, you ask, do I mean by this "Diet? Don't Try It" business?

Well, the word *diet* can simply mean "what we eat," but it can also mean "a regulated selection of foods." This is *diet* in the sense of something that people "go on" for a certain period, be it the Atkins Diet, the Grapefruit Diet, the Drinking Man's Diet, the Grandma's Chicken Noodle Soup Diet, the Impressive-Medical-Sounding-Name Diet, the Grocery Store Checkout Line's Cheap Little Booklet Diet, or one of the ten new diets people will think up tomorrow. When we go on diets, we tend to alter our eating habits for very limited periods, forcing ourselves to make unbalanced and unappetizing food choices that can't be sustained for the long run. (Come on, just how many days in a row did you really think you could eat cabbage soup for breakfast?) Almost all of these diets "work" for a time. We lose weight, but the real challenge comes when the diet is over, and real life starts up again.

We must resist such quick fixes just as we, as faithful Christians, resist the lure of cults and spiritual gurus. In fact, misguided dietary and religious enthusiasms both remind me of G. K. Chesterton's remark about heresies: every one of them overemphasizes some small truth at the expense of the whole, big body of truths. Sects and fringe denominations focus on a narrow interpretation of this or that Scripture verse or teaching, while ignoring its context, a vast array of other verses, and the weight of Tradition. Special diets latch on to a particular nutritional truth, but are blind to the bigger picture. Celery and broccoli are healthy, very low-calorie foods! (To Hades with all the others!) Too much dairy can cause problems for some people. (From now on, we will drink only soy!)

No, when it comes to diet, the basics, the tried-and-true staples, should form the healthy foundation of our bodily temples, just as tried-and-true spiritual staples (such as prayer, the sacraments, and the virtue of charity) should fortify our spirits.

Please bear my digression here on one very popular diet in particular, since it has become so popular a second time (and because I have my own personal vendetta against it!): the high-protein/low-carbohydrate diet was *the* thing in the 1970s. It was especially popular among bodybuilders to lose fat before competitions. For several reasons, the technique does lead to relatively rapid weight loss, but note that I said *weight*, and not necessarily fat, because you may say farewell to water and muscle tissue as well, and your scale won't tell you any different.

In a nutshell (yes, nuts are allowed) the second half of the word *carbohydrate* — *hydrate*, that is — refers to this nutrient's relation to water. If you limit your "carbs," you'll lose water, and therefore you'll weigh less on the scales. However, your brain feeds almost entirely on sugars, with carbohydrates being their primary source. If you deprive yourself of carbohydrates too severely, your brain (if you live long enough) will lead you to binge at some point in order to feed it properly. (Meanwhile, your body can also convert protein to carbohydrates — tapping, if necessary, into those precious stores within your muscles, thus making them smaller and weaker.)

I have my own "low-carb" story. In 1979, I entered the Teenage Mr. Illinois contest in Chicago. I went on a very low-carbohydrate diet for several weeks beforehand and got down to a very low bodyweight for me. After that contest and my inevitable carbohydrate binge, *I regained twenty pounds in one week.* I have not gone "low carb" again in the last twenty-eight years! The low-carb diet had already begun to go out of favor at that time, after some unfortunate individuals died from heart abnormalities following extremely low-carbohydrate liquid-protein diets. But, alas, by the late 1990s, there again, perhaps in a new and improved version, was the high-protein/low-carbohydrate fad once more. Ecclesiastes is right again: there is nothing new under the sun.[22] (But there is plenty of old, rancid wine for new wineskins.)

The Diet Worth Trying

Now it's time for the other sense of *diet,* according to its dictionary definition, "the usual food and drink of a person or animal; daily sustenance." This refers to our normal, daily, long-term eating regimen — to the ways we *habitually* eat, in the long run. This sense of diet holds the key to attaining leanness and to supplying the materials for our efforts at building muscle and cardiovascular endurance — for a lifetime. What we need to learn are realistic,

[22] Cf. Eccles. 1:9.

healthful, moderate (temperate), and enjoyable daily eating habits. What better day to start than today?

For the remainder of this chapter, I'll focus on some very basic principles to help you give your body the proper building materials you need to build strong and beautiful temples. In the next chapter, I'll provide some tips we can use to keep from taking in too much of some good things.

Pyramid Power?

There is great wisdom in the old notion of a "balanced" diet providing a variety of essential nutrients (proteins, fats, and carbohydrates at the larger "macronutrient" level, and vitamins and minerals at the smaller "micronutrient" level) in equal or "square" proportions. Back in my day, nutritionists conveyed this recommendation in terms of the "four basic food groups": 1) meat and nut products, 2) dairy products, 3) grains and cereals, and 4) fruits and vegetables. Take in foods from these four groups on a regular basis, we were taught, and go about your healthy business.

But with the passage of time, things tend to become more complicated (especially when group decision-making is involved), and we later arrived at the "food pyramid" with additional groups and a hierarchical arrangement. We were advised to eat more servings of the foods at the "base" of grains and cereals, and fewer servings as we work our way up through fruits and vegetables, dairy products, meats, eggs, and nuts, eventually arriving at the sparse little peak of oils, fats, and sugars.

Surely there's some wisdom to this pyramid, but there has been haggling and controversy over it, too. For example, cereals and grains have fallen somewhat out of vogue in some circles (see the low-carb diet, earlier), and some argue that fruits and veggies should occupy the position of honor at the pyramid's base. Some who argue this way use an evolutionary premise, basing their theories on speculations of a "Neanderthal" or "caveman" diet.[23] And it's not just nutritionists getting into the argument: the grain and produce industries have much to lose or gain, too.

Still, as imperfect as the pyramid may or may not be, and as un-pyramid-like as our diets may be in actual practice, do you personally know anyone suffering from dietary deficiencies such as scurvy, rickets, or a protein deficiency? As Christian author and nutritionist Gwen Shamblin argues so convincingly in her book *The Weigh Down Diet,* there's no need to be obsessed with nutritional balance. With the availability of such a huge variety of foods today, so many of them fortified with micronutrients, and with our tendency to eat so much more food than we actually need, most of us need not worry about being undernourished if our daily diets have any sense to them at all. Sometimes our body knows what it needs better than we do. We're wondrously crafted, after all. We tend *naturally* to desire a variety of foods that will satisfy our body's nutritional needs, if we let nature take its course.

What About Those Labels?

Although we need not obsess about every little vitamin and mineral our body needs, so long as we eat a sensible, well-rounded

---

[23] Something tells me, though, that grains and breads will never fall out of favor as the fundamental dietary and spiritual staple. The Old and New Testaments are full of metaphorical and literal references to bread, from the bread and wine brought forth by the great priest Melchizedek (Gen. 14:18) to the bread that rained down from heaven (Exod. 16:4). Jesus, the Bread of Life (John 6:35), advised us to pray for our daily bread (Matt. 6:11), and in the sacrament of the Eucharist, it is the ultimate priest, Jesus, who comes to us under the appearance of a wafer of bread.

diet, there's something to be said for acquiring a little more detailed knowledge about the basics of nutrition. For one thing, it
will make those mandated nutrition labels on food products more
understandable and useful.

One little game I like to play when people are examining labels
is to have them tell me the protein, carbohydrate, and fat content in grams (or just one or two of the three if I know the food
well), and I'll tell them the number of calories in a serving, within
a couple of calories or so. Alternatively, I'll have them tell me the
calories and one or two macronutrients (such as protein or fat
grams), and I'll tell them how many grams of carbohydrate the
food contains.

It's not a trick, just pretty simple math, because each gram of
protein has four calories, and so does each gram of carbohydrate,
while fat grams contain nine calories. A cup of 2-percent milk, for
example, has eight grams of protein (and thus, thirty-two calories),
eleven grams of carbohydrate (forty-four calories), and five grams
of fat (forty-five calories), making a total of 121 calories.

One little lesson we might observe from that aspect of label-
reading is that even though carbohydrates are often portrayed
as villains, *fats actually pack more than twice the potential body-
fat-building calories.* High levels of fat in the diet, especially saturated fat, are also linked to higher cholesterol levels and greater
risk for heart disease. So watch labels closely for fat. Choose foods
whose total calorie content is less than 30 percent fat, and compensate for higher-fat foods by eating them in smaller quantities
(there's the portion-size issue again) and eating lots of other low-
fat foods, too.

Back to milk, for example. At one point in my teens, I drank a
gallon of whole milk per day — that's 128 grams of fat, a ridiculous
and unhealthful amount. Later, when I learned of the value of a

low-fat diet, I switched to skim milk, but I wasn't so crazy about the flavor. In recent years, I've switched to 1-percent milk as a happy compromise. It has a little bit of fat (2.5 grams per cup), and I really like the flavor. I just don't keep drinking it 'til the cows come home.

Of course, all fats are not equal. Labels also differentiate between different kinds of fat, primarily between saturated, polyunsaturated, and mono-saturated fat. More-healthful mono-saturated fats come from nuts and from fattier fruits and vegetables, such as olives and avocados. Saturated fats come primarily from animal sources and should not be overdone. Polyunsaturated fats come primarily from vegetable sources. There are also some fats that contain healthful nutrients, such as the Omega-3 fatty acids in tuna and salmon. Conversely, it's a good idea to keep "trans" fats — which have been chemically altered by manufacturers — to a minimum. Check out a reputable college nutrition textbook (*not* a grocery-store pamphlet or paperback diet bestseller) for more straight scoop on the role of fats and other nutrients.

In the meanwhile, as you're checking for *low fat* content on those labels, keep your eyes open for *high fiber* content. Try not to go overboard on foods that have zero or only one gram of fiber per serving. Fiber keeps things moving through your system and provides for a sense of fullness that can keep you going strong and free from the urge to binge. Men would do well to take in twenty-five or thirty grams of fiber per day, and women at least twenty. Again, I'm not saying that you have to go around doing the math all the time. Just familiarize yourself with high-fiber foods that you like, and include them among your regular dietary staples.

While you're reading labels, one last detail to keep an eye out for is *portion size*. Note what the label describes as a serving size, and try to limit yourself to no more than one serving at one time.

(The numbers for that pint of ice cream don't look so bad until you note that the pint contains five servings!) Again, once you become familiar with the basic nutritional breakdown of various kinds of foods, you'll find that you'll rarely need to spend much time checking out those labels.

Supplements: Overfeeding the Overfed

What about the rows of pills, oils, and powders lining the shelves at our local pharmacy? Do we need to supplement our diets with special foods in order to achieve total fitness? I don't think so. A normal balanced diet is going to give us all the vitamins and minerals we need — and more, in most cases.

I used to be a vitamin junkie. In my teens, I took so many vitamin, mineral, protein, and other such supplements that I'm surprised people couldn't hear the pills jiggling when I walked. I used to amaze my peers by swallowing more than twenty assorted tablets in one gulp. Every day I'd pop a multivitamin, separate vitamin B complex, vitamin C, vitamin E, multiple brewer's yeast and desiccated-liver tablets, bone meal, kelp, lecithin, digestive enzymes, and other stuff I can't even remember, and this in addition to various protein and weight-gain milkshake concoctions, sometimes complete with ice cream, peanut butter, and whole eggs. (Yum!)

Then, at age seventeen, I attended a bodybuilding seminar by the reigning Mr. Universe, Mike Mentzer, who had actually studied university-level textbooks on nutrition — something practically unheard of for athletes in 1978. After hearing his lecture on the role of nutrition, I quit the mega-doses of vitamins and proteins, with no ill effects whatsoever.

Mentzer noted that high-intensity strength training provided the stimulus for muscle growth (as we saw in part II of this book).

During the rest period, the body taps into the nutrients we consume to build us back a little bigger and stronger. The kicker was that, in most cases, all the nutrients the body needs are available from a normal diet, and taking in more nutrients than necessary would in no way force the body to build itself any bigger or stronger. I'll bring up this issue again in the chapter on adolescents, since this is a fallacy very common among teenage boys and very eagerly promoted by those who peddle food supplements, but for now, I'll provide one example (and an amusing aside).

Mentzer argued that the popular use of protein supplements was unnecessary. These were days when the muscle magazines recommended 200 to 300 grams of protein per day for bodybuilders, whereas Mentzer recommended only fifty or sixty. (A glass of milk has eight grams of protein, and a large egg has six grams.) He provided mathematical calculations to show how little protein was necessary to fuel the growth of muscle tissue, and highlighted studies showing how the body simply excretes unneeded protein and water-soluble vitamins. (Some critics of supplementation have said that Americans produce the world's most expensive urine.)

Anyway, here's the amusing (to me, anyway) digression. Mentzer noted that muscle is only about 30 percent protein. The rest is water . . . "but they can't sell you water!" Well, that was 1978. Who would have thought that there would be so many expensive varieties of plain old water on the market today? (At least we don't think drinking it will force our muscles to become huge!) Some, however, do seem to endow water with almost magical powers, not in terms of muscle building, but in terms of fat loss. I'll talk about the use and misuse of water in one of the Muscle Mastery tip boxes.

I'd like to make one last note about dietary supplements. So-called "weight-loss supplements" and "ergogenic" or "performance-enhancing" dietary aids have much in common with those thousands of useless wonder diets. If you've lived a few decades and paid attention to the ads and infomercials, then you've seen many new wonder supplements for muscle building, weight loss, boundless energy, and even IQ- and memory-boosting, come and go. One of the wonder supplements that had its fifteen minutes of fame during my teenage years was quite appropriately called "Vitamin B-15." Shortly thereafter, fructose (fruit sugar) tablets were the rave, then came the miracle mineral of zinc, and a host of other marvel nutrients have come and gone since. They're popular for a little while and then fade out, making room for the next one. I advise a cautious skepticism regarding nutritional supplements. They do much more for their manufacturers' and advertisers' wealth than they'll ever do for your health.

Let's look next at what we should really be putting into our mouths. (And I don't think you'll find it a hard pill to swallow.)

Real Food Feeds!

A daily multivitamin isn't going to kill you. But I submit that by eating normal, everyday foods of the type that our grandmas and grandpas and their grandmas and grandpas ate, we can adequately nourish our bodies to support muscular growth, to replenish our bodies from cardiovascular workouts, and to stay lean and beautiful. And the key here, with real foods, is to take in the right amount, to find our own golden means. Milo can eat like a Milo and thrive mightily, but for you or me to do likewise could prove quite uncomfortable, or even fatal. But how do we make sure that we're not taking in too much of a good thing? Next we turn again to temperance — just the virtue to put gluttony in its place.

MUSCLE MASTERY TIPS AND FACTS #12

The Highs and Lows of Healthful Eating
There really is a lot of sense in that food pyramid, and one of its essential lessons is the wisdom of emphasizing foods that are high in carbohydrates and fiber (grains, cereals, vegetables, and fruits), and keeping to a relative minimum foods that are high in fats (such as fatty meats and oils). If you keep this simple principle in mind, and keep plenty of fruits, veggies, breads, and cereals around, it shouldn't be too hard to make high-fiber/low-fat eating a natural and desirable way to eat. Remember, we're after moderation, so you can still have the chocolate or the cheesecake, every day if you want, so long as you train yourself to acquire the temperance to savor and enjoy a most modest and sensible portion. *Bon appetit!*

Chapter 13

Goodbye to Gluttony

"Unless we first tame the enemy dwelling within us, namely, our gluttonous appetite, we have not even stood up to engage in the spiritual combat."
St. Gregory the Great

"He will have many masters who makes his body his master."
Seneca

It is perhaps with regard to temperance that virtue can be most clearly seen as a golden mean, as that pinnacle of perfection that embodies just the right balance. With diet, we can fall into the vice of *excess* food intake, and become too fat, or into the vice of *deficient* food intake — often through misguided and overzealous dieting — and become frail and gaunt, robbing ourselves of the important muscle tissue that helps keep our bodies healthy, vigorous, and beautiful.

Recall that building virtues entails three main things: 1) *knowing* good behaviors, 2) *choosing* good behaviors, and 3) the ongoing *practice* of those good behaviors. Our goal in this chapter, then, will be to train ourselves to desire the food choices that are best for us and to acquire a bag full of tricks to help us make those choices, until they become deeply ingrained habits — temperate, virtuous habits of total physical, mental, and spiritual fitness.

It's Not Nice to Fool Sister

Do you remember those old margarine commercials that ended with the line "It's not nice to fool Mother Nature"? It's a good line (if you keep in mind G. K. Chesterton's observation that nature is really our *sister*, sharing with us the same Father/Creator), for most of our attempts today at becoming lean through eating "diet" foods amount to attempts to fool our Big Sister. Granted, manufacturers are happy to come to our aid by sucking some of the fat and calories from our favorite chips and desserts, bestowing on us "light" and — lighter yet — "lite" foods and (heaven forbid) even beers. But when we consume these products, we're really only fooling ourselves.

These lite-ened products usually cost more, taste worse, and are less filling. End result? We pay more money, take in more calories, and enjoy it less. No wonder obesity rates in our country have climbed right along with the increased availability of "lite" foods. I myself remained more than thirty pounds overweight for two decades, while consuming all kinds of "lite" foods. The year I quit them was also the year I shed the thirty-five pounds.

Lite foods are antithetical to virtue in diet. Gwen Shamblin of the *Weigh Down Diet* nails it on the head when she says that attempts to alter foods in this way boil down to "making the food behave," instead of making ourselves behave (with God's help). Or to put it in our terms: habitually consuming "lite" foods is like trying to bestow the virtue of temperance upon our foods, rather than acquiring it ourselves! We think that if only *our foods* would obey the golden mean of nutritional balance, then we could intemperately consume them to our heart's content.

But food can't be virtuous — only we can. Moreover, building in ourselves the good habit of temperance is the *only* way to defeat gluttony and achieve long-term dietary health.

Gluttony: Foe of Temperance, Enemy of Leanness

Sorry, but I'm going to have to "get medieval on you" in this section. At least I'll be using a very old-fashioned concept. (When was the last time you heard a sermon on the sin of gluttony?) When the great medieval theologians, such as St. Albert the Great and St. Thomas Aquinas, addressed the virtues, those peaks of excellence, they also gave considerable thought to the vices that opposed them. The opposing vices of *temperance*, the virtue that keeps our sensual passions moral and in line with the dictates of right reason, are *lust* (for sexual passions), and *gluttony* (for food and drink). Let's take a good, hard look at gluttony, then, in the broad daylight (since it has a nasty habit of sneaking up on us in the dark, while we're watching television!).

We usually think of gluttony simply as the desire to eat too much food. But as St. Thomas shows, gluttony may also involve eating too quickly and ravenously (wolfing down our food); insisting on only fine and fancy foods prepared in a gourmet fashion; eating too often, when there is no real need; or simply by thinking excessively about food (making food an idol). Gluttony is not first and foremost about what we eat or how much of it, but about our having an "inordinate desire" for it, "not being regulated by reason."[24] St. Thomas even cites an old verse that sums up the various forms in which gluttonous behaviors are expressed: *hastily, sumptuously, too much, greedily, daintily.*

Take another look at the quotation from St. Gregory the Great at the start of this chapter. He knew so well that in hylomorphic beings of intertwined body and soul, things of the body affect quite directly things of the spirit. If we haven't mastered our gluttony, the "enemy within" that ravages our body, we're not in a very good position from which to build a spiritual life. Excessive desire for food takes our mind off higher things, excessive consumption makes us lethargic and bloated, rendering us less capable of charitable actions, and seeking excess comfort for our bellies makes us less apt to imitate Christ through suffering and sacrifice.

Note again that food itself is not the problem. We know that food is good — not just from our taste buds, but from the Bible. Jesus' first miracle, of course, transformed water to wine, and in

---

[24] *ST*, II-II, Q. 148, art. 1.

others, he multiplied loaves and fishes, feeding groups of thousands. In Matthew 15:11, he reminded the Pharisees, who enforced strict dietary laws, not to focus on what goes into a man's mouth, but what comes out of it — in other words, what he *wills*, not what he eats. (God reiterated the point to St. Peter in Acts, chapter 10.)

Jesus also showed us the value of food by abstaining from it (after all, it's only a sacrifice when we give up *good* things), such as when he fasted for forty days in the desert before the start of his social ministry. Following this example, Christ's Church continues to prescribe certain periods of total or partial fasting, from the hour before Mass to the disciplines of Lent. These practices show honor and respect to God, *and* they can help temper gluttony and build our capacities for temperance. Gluttony, then, is the foe not just of temperance but of justice, and not just of a healthy body but of a healthy soul.

Gutting Gluttony

What are some practical techniques for conquering gluttony by building up good, strong habits of dietary temperance? Let's put St. Thomas's categories to use. Consider first the gluttony of *too much*. Here is the bottom line that (if you'll excuse me) explains why our bottoms are so thoroughly lined with fat! We simply eat far too much food. The food industry has been training us over the years to "supersize it," thinking that we need more and more food at each meal while our poor (and once-little) stomach pouches are doing all they can to stretch themselves to accommodate. And have you seen the size of those soft-drink containers at the gas station? A family could take a bath in one!

Some try to fight back by eating larger volumes of "healthful," truly lower-calorie foods — like nibbling on a big bag of carrots or celery instead of a box of McNuggets. Well, I'm all for carrots or celery in moderation (and fried chicken as well), but I have a few reservations about this approach.

One, it still encourages a gnawing need to gnaw needlessly. Let's chew on this one in plain English. Carrots and celery are sent in to appease (and perhaps to slyly fool) our gluttonous need to munch. *Why not rather get rid of that need?*

Two, how many times have you snacked on a bag of tasteless but "healthful" food, only to go and get what you *really* want a little while later anyway? Purposely consuming high volumes of even those blessed low-calorie foods at the pyramid's base can wind up keeping us intemperate *and* fat. What we need to do instead is to wake up to our own bodies' real need for food quantity. In that spirit, here are some solid suggestions to counter the gluttony of *too much* (with some tips on conquering *hasty, greedy, dainty,* and *obsessive* eating as well):

GLUTTONY-BUSTERS

1. Order small sizes when ordering out, for food and for drinks. Before long, they'll make you feel as full and satisfied as larger sizes used to.

2. If you're given a very large serving at a restaurant, leave half on your plate, or ask for a to-go container and box it up *before* you start eating.

3. Speaking of restaurants, go ahead and order that dessert if you really want it. But share half of it with somebody else, or use the to-go-container trick.

4. Do you really need an "appetizer"? Most of us arrive at restaurants with appetites rarin' to go already. As Xenophon observed of Socrates: "He advised . . . to avoid appetizers that encouraged them to eat and drink what they did not want."

5. On the subject of sweets, when I dropped thirty-five pounds, I ate chocolate *every day*. My trick was to eat slowly and savor only one small piece of fine chocolate each day (usually a Lindt white- or milk-chocolate ball or a small piece of Ghiardhelli dark chocolate — each containing only seventy calories or so). Make it your hard-and-fast rule: only one piece per day!

6. Make it inconvenient to get to your food. Don't store a candy jar on your desk at work. (My chocolate stash remains out of sight in a closed file drawer.) Don't leave the foods out on your table when you eat at home. When having a snack such as chips, put a small amount in a container, then put the bag back in the pantry. Don't go back for more. Experiment over time to see if you can make the portion that satisfies you just a little bit smaller.

7. "Just eat a little bit less of everything." What frustrating advice! Doctors have been laying this one on their overweight patients for years. It's easier said than done, but it really is good advice. The trick to doing it is to be mindful of your eating habits (remember how virtue begins with *knowledge*?). Do you eat cereal for breakfast in the morning? Chances are that you load your bowl with more than what the box's side panel defines as a serving. Come on, who really gets sixteen bowls out of that box? All right, so you get about seven. Tomorrow, take a good look at that bowl, and put in just a little bit less. Keep this up over time until you reduce the quantity considerably, but to a level that still satisfies you. Apply this to all your food choices.

8. One serving only. Serve yourself a reasonable first portion, and eat like there won't be seconds: slowly, savoring each bite. Talk to your family. Sip water between bites. Train yourself to be content with firsts only, and soon you will be.

9. Always choose a small portion of a satisfying, unaltered, "real food" over an equal or larger portion of a "lite" food. (If you

find that you really prefer a lightened version of some food, there's no reason you can't have a reasonable portion of it instead.)

10. Forgive me for using the term "junk food" earlier in this book. Sweets and chips and the like are not really "junk" if eaten sparingly, as treats, in small doses. Go ahead and have that small bowel of delicious ice cream, rather than trying to substitute a quart of plain yogurt — and then heading back to the kitchen for some cookies too. Harking back to those nutritional labels, you may also consider training yourself to enjoy *less than* "one serving" of your special treats. For my favorite little gourmet chocolates, for example, three are listed as a serving, but as I noted, I always savor only one!

11. Don't buy really tempting treats at the grocery store. If you really want some ice cream, drive out to an ice cream parlor and get a small scoop of your very favorite. The cost and inconvenience will lead you to eat it less often, and savor it more. And here's a related tip: my wife and I live with a couple of young guys (our sons) who like their sweets, and they can get away with eating a lot more than we do. If they buy a load of special treats, I supply them with a plastic container and implore them to store them in their room — out of my sight, my mind, and my belly!

12. When someone offers you food at work or in some social setting, exercise the virtue of kindness: go ahead and have a bit. But eat a *little* less of your lunch, and don't go back for a second cookie, doughnut, or whatever. Then skip the day's chocolate ball!

13. Cut one course from your meals. You don't have to eat all four basic food groups (let alone an entire pyramid) at every meal. And if you go to a buffet (a near occasion for gluttony if there ever was one), don't feel the need to cover every square inch of your plate. (That's *square*, not *cubic* inches: don't build a pyramid *on* your plate, either!)

14. If you feel a little bit of hunger between meals, try slowly sipping a calorie-free soda, tea, or coffee, or nibbling a small mint such as a Tic-Tac. You might also try simply brushing your teeth when you're hungry; it will help put off your hunger, and you'll have minty-fresh breath between meals!

15. Better yet, try "offering up" the minor discomfort of your first pangs of hunger. And please note well, I'm advising *moderation* in this behavior, *not* self-starvation.

Don't Be a Glutton on a Diet

Have you ever dieted and found yourself constantly thinking about your next meal or snack, or even dreaming about it? Paradoxically, by "going on a diet," we often set ourselves up to fall into gluttony! In fact, strict dieting tends to make us focus too much on *ourselves* in general (and our bellies in particular), and such self-centeredness is contrary to the life of virtue and to life in Christ.

We also get into trouble when we think *too little* about eating — that is, when we don't use our human wills to *choose* what and when and how much to eat. Remember the line "Why does a man climb a mountain? Because it's there"? We often do the same with food. Why do we overeat? Because food is there, surrounding us. We don't even have to make a mindful effort to seek it out. So make it a point to keep food out of your sight, tucked away in the cupboards, and it will likely spend more time, if not out of your mind, then at least out of your mouth.

Dieting puts us at risk for gluttony in another way, too. The person who completely swears off pasta, or chocolate, or cheese, or cheesecake, or whatever the banned food may be, prepares the way for a *binge* that will quickly bring his "diet" to an end. So don't swear off pasta; just swear off covering a large plate with it.

Don't kiss chocolate goodbye; just start a one-small-piece-per-day club! Don't give up cheese or cheesecake; just make them small treats, and if necessary, rare treats.

Along the same lines, think of food quantity and portion control in the long term. If you should overdo it at one meal, take care to eat even a little less at the next meal, or skip or reduce your next snack. If you know you have a large family dinner coming up, eat a little less the meal before, and eat with reasonable gusto at the dinner, but when your modestly filled plate is cleared, don't get up again to reload.

Virtue Brings Rewards

St. Thomas told us that the virtue of temperance can lead to beauty. There is indeed a certain beauty when things are in their proper proportions. Even for food — just consider the sight of small portions of foods of various colors and textures, artfully arranged on a plate. Consider even more so the beauty of the human body when it is fed according to the reasonable dictates of health, rather than the bottomless demands of unchecked gluttony.

Another reward of virtue is happiness. I remember times in the past when my eating was out of control. Anything was fair game, *yet nothing tasted good!* But people who have mastered dietary temperance report that they truly *enjoy* and *savor* their food like never before. We should give thanks for this tasty fringe benefit!

✦✦✦

Let's recap a bit. In parts II, III, and IV of this book, we've considered the basic principles of the moral virtues of fortitude and temperance, as applied to the physical virtues of strength, endurance, and dietary self-mastery. Now it's time to proceed to the charioteer of the cardinal virtues, to see how the virtue of *prudence* can guide us in crafting the practical exercise routines that will take our bodies where we want them to go.

MUSCLE MASTERY TIPS AND FACTS #13

The Blast-Furnace Fallacy

I owe this terminology to Stamford and Shimer's *Fitness Without Exercise*. Although the phrase is theirs, it describes a phenomenon that many of us have seen, and some of us, myself included, have experienced. Some exercisers think that doing massive amounts of aerobic exercise can atone for all kinds of dietary sins. They act as if exercise turns their muscles into a blast furnace that will burn off not only bodily fat, but any kind of unhealthy effects that might arise through overeating. "Why not down a half-gallon of ice cream?" they might say, "I just ran ten miles." The truth is, doing aerobic exercise, even in the massive doses of a marathoner or triathlete, does not exempt you from dietary temperance and prudence. Worse, if you develop the habit of eating vast quantities of food because you think you can burn them off during your hour-long runs, you will gain fat quite rapidly when injury or busyness keeps you from your regular workout.

Part V

Prudence:
Putting Together Your
Total Fitness Workout Package

"Prudence is right reason applied to action."

St. Thomas Aquinas

Chapter 14

Building Your Own Strength Routine

*"To me indeed it seems that whatever is honorable,
whatever is good in conduct is the result of training,
and that this is especially true of prudence."*
Xenophon

*"As in the Olympic Games it is not the most beautiful
and strongest who receive the crown, but those who
actually enter the combat. For from those come the
victors, so it is those who act that win rightly
what is noble and good in life."*
Aristotle

"Prudence is right reason applied to action," says St. Thomas.

Xenophon chimes in (echoing Socrates) that prudence is a matter of *training*.

And old Aristotle tells us essentially that we can't win if we don't play.

So let's get in the game!

By now, we've covered basic theory on strength, endurance, and diet and connected them with the natural virtues of fortitude and temperance. Now it's time for *prudence*: the virtue that *gets the job done!* We will draw on this virtue to develop effective routines that will build your bodily strength in a safe and efficient way.

As you peruse these routines, please note how uncomplicated the whole program is. I simply suggest that you perform one set each of three basic compound exercises, along with another handful (about five) supplementary compound or isolation exercises. At a minute to a minute-and-a-half per set, and about the same amount of rest time between each set, the whole workout should be a simple, satisfying, and productive twenty-to-thirty-minute affair. Let's go.

An Ideal Whole-Body
High-Intensity Strength-Training Workout

I'm going to lay out several variations of strength-training workouts, starting with (as an example) my ideal routine. I consider a routine "ideal" when it achieves a perfect compromise between efficiency and comprehensiveness: allowing you to stimulate real growth in all the major muscles of your torso and limbs in less than a half-hour per week.

This first routine assumes that you have access to a well-equipped modern fitness center with a variety of strength-building exercise machines. I start with machines partly because they represent the ultimate in efficiency. Since machines have built-in paths of movement, it doesn't take much time to learn proper form. Machines with built-in weight stacks also take virtually no time to load or unload. With machines, you can also train alone with maximum intensity, in a minimum amount of time, with very little risk of injury. Machines are not at all necessary for maximizing muscular strength, but they're often simplest for beginners. I will also provide examples of other very good and productive routines that can be performed with the basic free-weight strength-training equipment of an inexpensive home gym, and finally, the most streamlined, yet still-profitable workout that can be performed with no equipment at all.

FUNDAMENTAL COMPOUND MACHINE EXERCISES

Exercise Machine	Primary Muscles Involved
Leg press:	Quadriceps, glutes
Chest press:	Pectorals, front shoulders, triceps
Pulldown, chin, or row:	Upper back, biceps

These exercises are the big boys of machine strength training, bringing into play nearly all the body's major skeletal muscles, plus many supporting muscles. With the *leg press*, the hamstrings and calves play supportive roles. Other muscles in the back play a stabilizing role in the *chest press*. The trapezius muscles that form a triangle between the shoulders and the neck, the rear deltoids of the back of the shoulder, the rhomboid muscles of the back, and many of the small muscles of the forearms and hands are also strongly affected by various *pulldown*, chinning, or rowing motions. Indeed, even the abdominal muscles get a vigorous workout from heavy pulldowns.

Let these exercises be the foundation of your workouts. Your fitness center should have trained staff who can show you how to use these machines properly, and how to adjust them to fit your body.

I recommend, especially if you're new to strength training, that you include another five exercises to round out your routine, choosing the ones from the following list that target the muscles you'd like to build or tone. Be sure to follow the instructions on each machine, and ask gym staff for help if you have any confusion.

A SAMPLE MENU OF SUPPLEMENTAL MACHINE EXERCISES

Exercise Machine	Primary Muscles Involved
Hip and back:	Hip and back (you guessed?)
Leg curl:	Hamstrings
Standing or seated calf:	Calf and soleus (under the calf)
Hip abductor/adductor:	Hip abductors and adductors
Dip:	Pectorals, triceps, front shoulders
Overhead press:	Front shoulders, triceps
Shoulder shrug:	Trapezius and neck
Lateral raise:	Side deltoids (shoulder)
Biceps curl:	Biceps
Abdominal:	Abdominals
Lower-back extension:	Lower back
Neck:	Front, sides, back of neck
Grip machine:	Forearms and hands

You don't really need to do more than eight exercises during each workout. But over time, you may want to vary the supplemental exercises you perform. Perhaps you'd like to emphasize a particular body part for a month or so, and then move on to emphasize something else. That's just fine. You can also vary them at random, performing whichever exercise sounds appealing on a particular day in the gym.

I recommend doing these supplemental exercises in the order listed, or close to it. (Give chapter 9 another try for a refresher on the reasons why.) And please remember that even in our sample menu of exercise, modest portion size still applies.

By performing some version of the big three fundamental compound exercises in each workout, you won't be committing a sin of omission for any of the major muscle groups. With each workout, be sure to include "a leg, a push, and a pull" — that is, one major compound leg exercise, one major compound chest exercise, and one major compound back exercise. Those are the nutritious mashed potatoes of our workouts. Anything else is gravy, a tasty extra, but not to be overdone.

A Rock-Solid Free-Weight
Routine for a Rock-Solid You

Barbells and dumbbells have been building big, strong muscles and bones for over a hundred years now, and they still get the job done. Most commercial fitness centers still boast a wide array, and they remain the most practical choice for a home gym. Use them with caution, however. It can be very dangerous to perform some exercises alone, such as a barbell bench press, so be sure to have your workout buddy or a friendly stranger standing by to "spot" you. You can also use "power racks" — safety bars to support the weights — to make at-home lifting safer. It's also possible to build fine, strong muscles with barbells and dumbbells alone, even without a bench. Here's a sample workout.

FUNDAMENTAL COMPOUND
FREE-WEIGHT EXERCISES

Exercise	Primary Muscles Involved
Squat or deadlift:	Quadriceps, glutes, lower back
Bench or overhead press:	Pectorals, front shoulders, triceps
Barbell row or chin-up:	Upper back, biceps, forearms

These fundamentals are akin to the machine fundamentals described earlier, and again they boil down essentially to "a leg, a push, and a pull." The *squat* is a deep-knee bend with a barbell on the shoulders. I recommend that you get help from a professional trainer or a friend with true expertise in weight training to learn the proper performance of this exercise. Because squats can be dangerous and cumbersome if you're working out alone without a power rack, I include the *deadlift* as an alternative. Here, the bar starts on the ground before you, resting at your shins. You bend over, bending your knees, and with a straight back, grab the bar and slowly stand up straight with it. Again, I recommend you seek in-person advice, or at least study the illustration that came with your barbell set, for further guidance in proper performance.

The *bench press* can be performed with a barbell or with a dumbbell in each hand. Do each one slowly, and under control. Do not perform barbell bench presses if you're alone and aren't lifting inside a safety rack. I also urge you to seek out more advice in the performance of barbell or dumbbells bent-over rows. It's important that your back remain flat or slightly arched, and not hunched. An alternative to the rows is a *pulldown motion*, which can be done with the overhead pulleys often included with home gyms or power racks. Another alternative is the tried-and-true *chin-up* or *pull-up* if you have a bar (or the perfectly situated jungle-gym bar or tree branch — but be careful!).

A SAMPLE MENU OF
SUPPLEMENTAL FREE-WEIGHT EXERCISES

<u>Exercise</u>	<u>Primary Muscles Involved</u>
"Good mornings":	Lower back, hamstrings
One-legged dumbbell calf raise:	Calves and soleus
Barbell or dumbbell shrugs:	Trapezius and neck
Dumbbell lateral raises:	Medial deltoids (side shoulder)
Barbell or dumbbell curls:	Biceps and forearms
Dumbbell kickbacks:	Triceps
Sit-ups, crunches, or frog kicks:	Abdominals
Barbell wrist curls:	Forearms
Neck harness work:	Back, side, front of neck

"Good mornings" are performed with a barbell across the shoulders. Being careful not to let the bar roll down to your neck, keep your knees slightly unlocked, and bend forward at the waist with a flat or slightly arched (not hunched) spine. Bend over as far as possible without losing your balance; then return to the upright position. When done right, these will enhance flexibility and strength in your lower back and hamstrings and make you less susceptible to all-too-common lumbar-disc and other lower-back injuries.

For *one-leg calf raises*, stand on a wooden block about four inches high on the ball of one foot. Hold one dumbbell with the hand on the same side of your body as the foot that you're using. Stand as high as you can on your toes, and sink as low as comfortably possible. Repeat throughout the set, and then change legs. In the old bodybuilding lingo of my youth, every musclehead strived after "diamond-shaped" calves. The simple one-legged calf raise can help turn those spindly lower legs into some real gems.

Next, let's move up, way up the body to those trapezius muscles that slope between the shoulders and the neck. For *shrugs*, stand up straight with your arms completely extended at your side for dumbbells or slightly in front for a barbell. Simply raise your shoulders as high as possible, as if trying to touch your ears. Strong trapezius muscles are very helpful for any task of daily life requiring you to lift and move an object with your arms. With all the televisions and sofas I've hoisted over the years, I've been glad to have trained trapezius muscles for the task.

For *curls*, stand with your arms extended, palms up, and curl them all the way up while keeping your elbows in essentially the same position.

For *hammer curls*, use a neutral grip with your thumb at the top, as if you were using a hammer.

For *dumbbell kickbacks*, bend at your waist with a dumbbell in one hand and your elbow tucked at your side. Move the weight behind you and up until your elbow locks. Return and repeat. (This will help you build "horseshoe" triceps, as the lingo goes.)

For *sit-ups*, keep your knees bent and anchored under a barbell or couch. Do not lie completely back down. Just go down until your lower back touches and go up until you feel the tension on the abdominals releasing. Although sit-ups can be made progressively more intense by increasing the angle of a sit-up board (the higher the feet, the greater the intensity), by holding progressively heavier barbell plates or dumbbells in front of your chest, or by performing them more slowly, I wouldn't worry about doing sit-ups to complete failure. Intensifying this exercise can be rough on the lower back, and most of us are probably not interested in making our abs as huge as possible![25]

For *crunches*, you start like a sit-up, but merely curl up from your middle without raising your upper body around the axis of your hip joints. You may move but a few inches. Don't worry — abdominals have a small range of motion.

For *frog kicks*, sit leaning slightly back with your hands on a chair or a bench. Extend your feet out, and then bring your knees up to your chest as high as you can. You'll feel these in the abdominal muscles down low below the navel. (Oh yes, we used to talk about "washboard" abdominals, but who uses washboards anymore? Now they're called the "six-pack.")

A great advantage to barbells and dumbbells is variety, and indeed I've given you but a small sample of the movements that can be done with them. If these are to be your strength-building tools of choice, check out some good books illustrating free-weight exercises, and then apply the same principles I gave you for machine workouts: choose a few, maybe five or so, to supplement your three fundamental movements. And switch them up as you see fit.

Bare-Bones Basics:
Freehand Strength-Building Exercises

Even if you don't have the desire or the means to join a gym or buy some weights, you can obtain some strength-building benefits

---

[25] In fact, as a general rule, for your abdominal exercises, I advise you to focus more on slow repetition speed, perfect form, and feeling the movement in your muscles than on using increasingly heavier loads. The abdominal muscles are also strengthened indirectly from using increasing loads on high-intensity back exercises like the pulldown and pullover.

using your body, or objects around your home, as resistance. These "freehand" exercises are also known as *calisthenics*, deriving from the Greek words *kalli*, for "beauty" and *sthenos*, for "strength." When properly done, they should enhance both form and function!

FUNDAMENTAL COMPOUND
CALISTHENIC EXERCISES

Exercise	Primary Muscles Involved
Deep knee bend:	Quadriceps, glutes
Push-up:	Pectorals, front shoulder, triceps
Chin-up or sit-up:	Back and biceps (or abdominals)

Bear in mind, you cannot perform full-blown high-intensity strength training with most of these exercises, because you won't be able to increase the weight you're lifting, but your muscles can still derive some benefit, and there are still some ways you can progress and increase intensity. For the deep knee bends (squats without a barbell), you may want to extend your arms in front of you as you descend slowly to your lowest comfortable squatting position, with no bouncing at the bottom! Intensity can be increased by descending lower as your flexibility builds, by performing more repetitions in subsequent workouts, and by performing your repetitions more slowly. (The last two principles apply to all these freehand exercises.)

Push-ups can be done in the standard military manner by most men, and by women with especially good upper-body strength. Others may need to keep their knees on the ground to reduce the intensity. Intensity can be increased by slightly raising your feet by resting them on a low object, by placing each hand on a book, or by using special hand-held grips (found at many sporting-goods stores) that allow a greater range of motion.

I talked about *chin-ups* (also called pull-ups) before. Since not everyone has access to a bar for chinning, an alternative fundamental freehand exercise (although it obviously does not work the same muscles), is the sit-up. Other alternative exercises pretty much parallel those for barbells and dumbbells, and some can be done with light household objects, stones, buckets, or what have you. It's pretty hard to be systematic about improving on these exercises. But if you're seeking a minimal workout to keep your muscles in reasonably good condition, freehand exercises far exceed the exercise we give our free hands by operating a remote control or digging to the bottom of the potato-chip bag!

The simplicity of these exercises allows them to be done if you're traveling, or are so overwhelmed by other activities that you can't make it to the gym for a while. And further, since they're less demanding and can be done for a longer period and for more repetitions, they're more amenable to doubling up with spiritual exercises while you train — for example, praying, listening to devotional music, thinking about spiritual reading, rehearsing memorized catechetical information, or planning some acts of kindness to be done when you've finished your workout.

◆◆◆

Simple enough? If you're new to strength training, it can be daunting to open up that set of barbells and dumbbells for the first time, let alone to step into a gym full of clanging weights and buff, sweaty gym rats. But I hope I've helped to demystify the world of practical strength training for you. There's no complicated secret formula that only veteran bodybuilders know. You don't have to do every exercise under the sun, and you don't have to work out from sunup to sundown! Remember that just a few minutes once per week spent performing "a leg, a push, and a pull" will go very far in building a strong, muscular foundation for your temple. Add another handful of supplementary exercises to each workout, and in time, your temple will stand sturdy and complete.

The next chapter will provide more detail to demonstrate how your actual strength and endurance workouts can be laid out in a weekly schedule. I'd like to conclude this chapter, though, with some specific pointers to keep in mind once you actually get into the game and put your muscles to work.

Practical Strength-Training Guidelines: A Summary (with a nod to their underlying theoretical principles)

1. Work each exercise through a full range of motion. (Form)

2. Perform slow and smooth repetitions. You don't have to look at a clock or be exact, but think in terms of about two-second positives and four-second negatives. (Duration, intensity)

3. Breathe naturally, and try not to contract muscles that are not involved in the exercise. Gripping intensely while performing a leg press, for example, can cause an unwanted temporary increase in your blood pressure. (Form)

4. Perform one set only of eight to twelve repetitions per exercise. (Duration, frequency)

5. Don't stop your set until you actually fail during a repetition, or until your last repetition was so difficult that you doubt you can perform another. (Intensity)

6. If you successfully perform twelve repetitions today, increase the weight by about 5 percent or so in your next workout, and work your way back to twelve repetitions with that new weight in subsequent workouts. (Progression, intensity)

7. Start with the fundamental exercises, and work your way down to the supplemental, as you move from larger to smaller muscle masses. (Order)

8. Take a minute or two to regain your breath between the exercises, so your muscles fail before you run out of breath. If you take turns with a partner, this will work out just about right — if you don't dilly-dally much. (Rest, intensity)

9. Go put away the weights, and don't do it again for a week! (Rest, frequency)

Let's move next to the practical aspects of incorporating *both* high-intensity strength training *and* cardiovascular endurance training into a workable weekly workout routine.

MUSCLE MASTERY TIPS AND FACTS #14

The Spot-Reducing Fallacy

Many people think that to reduce the fat from your stomach or thighs, you must work those specific muscles — and work them like there's no tomorrow. It's just not true. In *Fit or Fat*, Covert Bailey explains that fat does not "belong" to the muscle group it overlies; rather, it "belongs" to the whole body. When you gain fat, *your body decides where to put it.* The usual location for men is the abdomen and for women, the hips and thighs. It later works its way through the rest of the body, and even the face. When you lose fat through proper exercise and diet, the body tends to rid itself of fat in the opposite order, saving its favorite deposits for last. *You do not alter this process by working the specific muscles under the fat.* (Yep, all those abercisers on TV infomercials are a waste of time and money.) Any muscle you develop will help your body burn calories and reduce fat throughout the body, but you can't tell your body where to remove it by your choice of exercises. Running, for example, uses primarily the legs, but take a look at a serious distance runner, and you'll see that it has trimmed his waist (or her hips) much more than endless sit-ups or repetitions on the "thigh blaster" ever could.

Chapter 15

Simple Sample Weekly Workouts

*"But he approved of taking as much hard exercise as
is agreeable to the soul; for the habit not only ensured
good health, but did not hamper care of the soul."*
Xenophon, describing Socrates

*"And he shall make a strong covenant
with many for one week."*
Daniel 9:27

Year after year, fitness centers swell with new members in early January. (You can barely find a parking place where I go.) But even before February hits, the crowds have begun to thin as the "resolutionists" drift away from their well-intentioned, but short-lived New Year's vows.

But why do they stop? I believe it's for two major reasons. First, because they find the routines they're taught (or the ones they glean from fitness magazines) to be complicated and time-consuming. They're told to perform too many sets of too many exercises requiring too much time on too many days of the week. The second reason is they haven't been taught to pursue total strength training as virtue: part of a hylomorphic approach to whole-person fitness — body, soul, and mind.

Well, you know better now, don't you? So, as you near the end of this book and prepare to set out on your own quest for total fitness, I hope I've given you the tools and the understanding to avoid the plight of the resolutionists!

What is now required on your part is *perseverance*, which is part of the virtue of fortitude. After having acquired the knowledge of what to do, you must get down to the brass tacks of actually doing it, week after week!

A Week to Get Strong

Workout systems are usually laid out week to week, and I find that it works best to do my strength session on the same day every week (Saturday mornings, for more than two decades now), so that it becomes part of my typical routine. Find the day that works for you, but do feel free to change it by a day or two here or there, rather than skipping workouts entirely.

And don't necessarily discount Sunday! Sometimes I do a formal aerobics workout on Sunday, before or after Mass. Nervous about violating the Sabbath? Don't worry; listen to Pope Pius XII: "The Church does not forbid sports on Sunday. She looks upon it kindly, provided that Sunday remains the Lord's day, the day of repose of body and soul."[26] And Sunday is an especially good day to schedule in fun and calorie-burning activities for the entire family.

Remember again the call to moderation. If you must miss a workout, or two or three, you needn't throw in the towel. We shouldn't think of exercise, or diet for that matter, in all-or-nothing terms. If you fall off the wagon, climb back on and carry on from where you were.

Pay attention to time of day too. Are you more of a night owl than a lark? Is your lunch hour, or just after work, more practical for you?

Exercise your ingenuity to make your exercise schedule fit you to a *T*.

Let's lay out a sample weekly schedule, incorporating strength training, aerobics, and normal daily activities in keeping with the principal principles previously presented (sorry about that). Modify it in any way you see fit — or scrap it and start from scratch. But do make a schedule for yourself; it will be a big aid to perseverance.

---

[26] Cited in Robert Feeney, *A Catholic Perspective: Physical Exercise and Sports* (San Francisco: Ignatius Press, 1995).

Simple Sample Weekly Workouts

SAMPLE LIFTING, AEROBIC, AND
NORMAL ACTIVITY WEEKLY SCHEDULE

Saturday:	Lift (20 minutes)
Sunday:	Rest
Monday:	Aerobics (20 minutes)
Tuesday:	Rest
Wednesday:	Aerobics (20 minutes)
Thursday:	Rest
Friday:	Aerobics (20 minutes)

All right, there's an example of a basic, bare-bones-minimum week that can move you along on the road to total fitness. It entails twenty minutes of strength training and sixty minutes of aerobic training, less than an hour-and-a-half total investment. Also, on the rest days and on the workout days, "house aerobics" can be added into the mix on a very regular basis. I don't count the time for the normal activities because those kinds of activities should be done anyway. That's just life! There can be countless variations on this theme. You can vary the aerobic exercises at will, and you can vary the days of the week in which you train. If you have no equipment and do not belong to a gym, you could walk vigorously, or run, or ride an ordinary bicycle all three times if you prefer.

If you enjoy aerobic exercise, have the time, and would like to lose a little weight, you can do longer sessions. I found that thirty-five-minute sessions really did the trick for me. You could also do aerobic workouts more often than three times per week — even daily if it seems to work for you.

Too Much of a Good Thing?

But be careful not to overtrain. How do you tell if you're overtraining? One very simple indicator is your performance in your strength-training workouts. If your strength plateaus or declines, if you're not making small, but regular strength increases in at least some of your exercises, despite giving full effort to your high-intensity sets, you may be doing too much aerobic training, hampering your muscles' ability to recuperate and supercompensate. In that case, try gradually cutting back on the frequency and duration of your aerobic sessions until your strength-training efforts are again going strong.

But do bear in mind, the three basic twenty-minute aerobic sessions I've suggested as a minimum are very unlikely to produce overtraining. It's when you're upping the ante with longer or more frequent aerobic sessions that you'll have to be careful not to exceed the golden mean.

Now, here's a more detailed sample schedule using machines:

TWO WEEKS' WORTH OF STRENGTH WORKOUTS

Week 1		Week 2	
Exercise	Pounds x reps	Exercise	Pounds x reps
Leg press	200 x 12	Leg press	210 x 9
Leg curl	80 x 10	Leg curl	80 x 11
Calf raise	210 x 9	Calf raise	210 x 10
Chest press	140 x 8	Chest press	140 x 9
Lat. pulldown	150 x 11	Lat. pulldown	150 x 12
Seated press	120 x 12	Seated press	125 x 8
Curl machine	70 x 10	Curl machine	70 x 11
Ab machine	70 x 8	Lateral raise	70 x 9

In our example, I've chosen eight machine exercises that work the majority of the body's major muscles. Please, *nota bene*, the weights listed are arbitrary. You'll have to determine your own proper starting weights. Here's one way. Select a poundage that you can lift in perfect form with moderate difficulty and perform as many repetitions as possible. You'll be shooting for a range of eight to twelve repetitions. If you find you can do only four or five, let's say, decrease the poundage as necessary in your *next workout*, so that you fail somewhere between eight and twelve repetitions. Conversely, if you can do more than twelve, use a heavier weight *next time*. In a few workouts, you'll find the proper poundages for the various exercises.

Also, in the previous chart, I've used the same machines both weeks to illustrate how you might expect to progress. In practice, once you become familiar with the equipment, you can throw in some different exercises from week to week for variety.

You'll notice from the chart that when twelve repetitions are achieved, it's time to raise the poundage in the next workout. Before you reach twelve, you should strive to add an additional repetition or two with the same poundage. Is this clear? If not, you might want to take another peak at chapter 3, where we first discussed the principle of *progression*.

Now, let's say you're a minimalist and a time-efficiency expert who doesn't care for either strength training or aerobic training. Wow! Can I make any fitness suggestions that might appeal to you? Here's my bare-bones recommendation:

ULTRA-BARE-BONES MINIMUM FITNESS REGIMEN

Saturday:	Lift (10 minutes)
Sunday:	Rest
Monday:	Rest
Tuesday:	Rest
Wednesday:	Rest
Thursday:	Rest
Friday:	Rest

A few things to keep in mind for this scenario. First, most, if not all, of those days of "rest" from formal fitness activities, should be loaded with normal physical activities, both at home and on the job. You'll want to refer back to chapter 11 for some examples, and to think up some of your own as well. Without formal aerobic activities to burn off extra calories, the pressure will really be on for a tighter diet and more extensive normal physical activity, but it can be done!

So, in a nutshell, for the ultimate bare-bones minimum, on one day per week, do only three strength-training exercises — a major compound leg exercise and a compound pushing and a compound pulling exercise for the upper body (such as a squat or leg press, standing or bench press, and a pulldown, chin, or row of some kind — remember "a leg, a push, and a pull"). If you're also willing to devote another twenty minutes per week to building up your cardiovascular system, then the next day, do only one twenty-minute aerobic session (but no slacking off). Your formal training investment will be a mere thirty minutes per week; the other days of the week, go about your business, but be sure to get in at least thirty minutes of mild normal activities each day.

Every Little Bit Helps

Do you recall the all-or-nothing, dichotomous thinking I described as so fatal to total fitness pursuit? When it comes to putting into practice these principles of strength training, endurance training, and sensible diet, rather than thinking you have to go full-bore all the time or you might as well quit, remind yourself that "every little bit helps." The strength routine itself is quite little in terms of time investment. And even brief, mild aerobic sessions can have a major impact on your fitness and leanness, if you do them often enough. Small things such as climbing that flight of stairs or parking your car a little farther from the entrance can add up if you do enough of them on a regular basis.

The same applies to diet. If you overindulge, don't chuck the whole approach out the window — just rein in your portion size at your next meal or snack. Little things such as leaving a few bites on your plate or splitting a doughnut with a coworker rather than having one or two on your own, will add up over time. *Every day* there will be opportunities for making very small contributions to your quest for total fitness. Keep putting them together over time, and lo, what a temple you'll have!

What Twenty Weeks of HIT Can Do

In this chapter, I've tried to focus on the basic fundamental training principles to keep things simple in helping you craft your own fitness routines, but perhaps it would also help you to see a more detailed example of the workouts and the results obtained from one real person's total fitness regimen of strength training, aerobic training, and diet. If you visit http://cbass.com/Vost2.htm, you can see a detailed description of my own program and what it did for me. Check it out now, or save it for the end. Either way, I truly hope these methods will produce some gratifying results in your own pursuit of bodily, mental, and spiritual perfection. And speaking of results, that's what the next chapter is all about.

MUSCLE MASTERY TIPS AND FACTS #15

Greece's Greatest Mind
Ponders Greece's Greatest Body

"It doesn't follow that if ten pounds of meat is too much and two too little for a man to eat, the trainer will order him six pounds, since this also may be too much or too little for him who is to take it; it will be too little, for example, for Milo, but too much for a beginner in gymnastics. The same with running and wrestling; the right amount will vary with the individual." — Aristotle, *Nichomachean Ethics*, *Bk.* II, ch. 5

Chapter 16

The Virtue of Results

"I am the way, and the truth, and the life."
John 16:4

*"Suppose, for example, that in talking to an athlete,
I said, 'Show me your shoulders,' and then he
answered, 'Look at my jumping weights.' Go to,
you and your jumping weights! What I want
to see is the effect of the jumping weights."*
Epictetus

Some of the wisest men in history, such as Aristotle and St. Thomas Aquinas, have proposed a "correspondence theory" of truth, according to which an idea or statement is true when it corresponds to — is in agreement with — reality. Isn't that common sense?

We see that common sense at work in the modern scientific method. Hypotheses are formed and then put to the test through careful experimentation in the search for valid cause-and-effect relationships. If a training technique is believed to produce rapid growth in strength, then, by darn, it actually should do so in real live people! Now, I'm not suggesting that readers go out and hire some researchers and recruit a control group to put these fitness methods to the test. (That might be scientific, but you might question my common sense.) No, the research subjects we'll use to test the truth of the principles in this book, will, of course, be us.

Or, in other, simpler words, the proof will show in our shoulders. To borrow from Epictetus, we will know that our efforts at total fitness training have been successful, not by our new running shoes or workout gear or barbell set or gym membership card, but by the actual changes in our own bodies, by how we look, by our function and our form. I'm going to focus in this chapter on the bodily results of our training — how we can identify and gauge them.

Lift It Up, Write It Down

One good way to help evaluate your results is to put them down on paper, where you can return to them and track them over time.

During periods of intense training for power-lifting competitions, I used dated calendar books to record each workout, and tracked my major competitive lifts on graph paper (and later on a computer spreadsheet). You won't need such elaborate record keeping, but here are a few things you might want to do to monitor your results.

Weighing In

If weight control is one of your goals, weigh yourself without clothing first thing every morning on your bathroom scale. Aim for gradual and steady weight loss, not exceeding a pound or two per week. If you lose faster than that, you're most likely losing muscle. Also, don't worry about minor day-to-day fluctuations. Even if your weight is relatively stable, you may come to see regular weekly variations of a pound or two on different days. (I tend to be my heaviest on Saturday mornings because we like to go out for Italian food on Friday nights!) So compare your weights from week to week.

Those scales can be a great, objective way to maintain awareness of the positive results of your training — and help keep extra pounds from sneaking up on you. But remember that scales do not tell the whole story. They tell you pounds, but not pounds "of what" — fat or water or muscle. Another alternative is to measure your waistline every morning. For women, daily hip measurements will also give an accurate reflection of progress. But remember, if you choose to measure, be happy with small and gradual reductions.

Stronger Than the Week Before

Barbells and strength-training machines provide built-in result-measuring devices — the greater a weight you can move in good form, the stronger you've become! They also provide an indirect way to be sure that the weight you're losing isn't muscle: if you're actually *losing* strength from one workout to the next, you may be dropping bodyweight too rapidly.

In your first year or so of training, you should expect small, but steady gains in your strength. As we saw in the sample schedules earlier, for most workouts, you should strive to add a repetition or two, or a small weight increase on each of your exercises, and in virtually every workout, you should show some improvement in at least some of your exercises. Fight the tendency to cheat on your form just to show "improvement" in repetitions or numbers, though. In fact, just showing better form from one workout to the next can be an indication of improvement.

Cinch That Belt

Your clothing will tend to be very honest in letting you know how you're shaping up. For most of my adult life, I've weighed a little over 200 pounds at 5 foot, 9 inches, and during a peak period of creatine craziness, I once peaked out at 234 pounds. Most of the time, I wore size 36-waist pants, although I did own some 38s and even a 40 or two. (In fact, when I was measured for a kilt for a Highland Games competition in 1999, my waist was over forty inches, which is a cardiac risk factor for men.) As I came to my senses and starting practicing the virtues of total physical fitness in 2006, my goal was to wear size 34-waist pants. Five months later, I was wearing 32s for the first time in my adult life, and I had to buy a whole new wardrobe! Now I *must* stay in these smaller pants, or my wife won't let me hear the end of it.

Breathing Easy

It will also be easy to monitor the results of your aerobic training. You'll be able to walk or run or bike or swim or do the machines faster, harder, and longer, with less huffing and puffing. And if you're using cardiovascular machines such as a treadmill, a bicycle, an elliptical trainer, or a stair climber with adjustable intensity and electronic readouts, you'll be able both to note progression and to keep track of time, distance, and calories burned. A similar tactic for outdoor walking, running, biking, or swimming is to strive to knock just a few seconds or so off your total time to cover a given distance. Did you run two miles in 21:12 today? Next week, shoot for 21:11 or faster. (Of course, improvement can't go on forever, and your times will eventually stop improving much, but you'll be maintaining a fitness level much higher than what you started with.)

As far as the "house aerobics" or normal-daily-activity training goes, you'll be able to see those results as well, in cleaner countertops, fuller linen closets, neatly trimmed lawns, organized garages, slimmer dogs, and a more energetic *you*.

All right, soon you'll have some shoulders worth showing. But what about the spiritual results of your training? You want your soul to "show" the virtues of fitness, too, after all. Let us now give the highest of virtues their rightful due.

MUSCLE MASTERY TIPS AND FACTS #16

On "Split" Routines

Should you split up your strength workouts — that is, work only certain parts of your body during a given workout, but work out multiple days per week? HIT strength training experts are — you guessed it — "split" on the question. Some, for example, Arthur Jones and Dr. Ellington Darden, strongly favor whole-body routines only. Others, such as Mike Mentzer and former Mr. Olympia Dorian Yates, have shown that incredible muscularity can be built by training each muscle only once a week, but splitting up the workouts into two, three, or even four days per week. If you're extremely serious about strength training, and enjoy spending time in the gym, by all means try splitting up your sessions. You might want to tack your brief aerobic workouts on to the end, since you'll be in the gym or your own workout area anyway. Although I endorse whole-body training myself, since it's more time-efficient, I do tend to compromise a bit. Sometimes on an aerobics training day, I'll throw in only one strength exercise, working a muscle I didn't train on Saturday — something small such as my calves or neck.

Conclusion

Faith, Hope, and Charity: Exercising the Ultimate Virtues

"By faith, we believe in God and believe all that he has revealed to us and that Holy Church proposes for our belief. By hope we desire, and with steadfast trust await from God, eternal life and the graces to merit it. By charity, we love God above all things and our neighbors as ourselves for the love of God. Charity, the form of all the virtues, "binds everything together in perfect harmony" (Col. 3:14).

Catechism of the Catholic Church, par. 1842-1844

At the beginning of this book, I said I wanted to create a "theology of bodybuilding." Well, you can't have a "theology" of *anything* by treating natural things (even virtues) only. If our efforts are to bear full fruit — if physical fitness is to make us not only strong and virtuous but also more ready for heaven — then we must finally consider the strength of God's arm: the power of his supernatural grace working on and in us.

The natural virtues can help prepare us for grace, but they can't replace it. And so we must address the *theological virtues:* faith, hope, and charity. Where the natural virtues help us perfect our human natures, the theological virtues *transform* our human nature, and enable us to participate in divine life. Where the natural virtues can be developed by our knowledge, hard work, and perseverance, the theological virtues are a pure gift from God, infused directly into our souls.[27] They are the highest of the virtues, and they will lead us to the highest goal of hylomorphic fitness: salvation.

Faith and Fitness

Faith describes our belief in God and in all that he has revealed to us. It also entails a desire to know his will. God reveals his will to us through the scriptures and through the teachings of his Church. We have seen in these pages that God has told us through

[27] See CCC, par. 1813.

the scriptures themselves, and through the words of theological doctors and holy pontiffs of his Church, that the care and perfection of our physical bodies is a good thing, an endeavor that does honor to his Holy Spirit. God has also revealed himself in every element of his creation, including the wonderful workings of our own bodies and our capacity for reason.

St. Thomas Aquinas tells us that whereas hope and charity reside in the will, the virtue of faith resides in the human *intellect*. This means that in one sense, faith comes first.[28] Both the hope to share in eternal life with God and the desire to direct our love toward him presuppose that we know him. While we are here on earth, unaided reason alone cannot know the triune God, so we need the guidance of faith provided through God's revelation. (In the next life, direct knowledge of God will replace the need for faith.)

How, then, does the virtue of faith bear on our quest for total fitness? Taking St. Thomas's lead, we should look to the role of the intellect, to the most fundamental ideas that guide our lives. Faith in God is *not* required to tend to the needs of the body, the physical dimension of the hylomorphic equation. The quest for the ultimate body, after all, is near the top of the list of secular, hedonistic values. Indeed, for some fitness zealots, muscle is their Mammon — a false god diverting their thoughts and actions from the one true God.

Because we tend to associate the flesh with faithless folk, and because faith resides in the non-material intellect, we usually consider faith's role only in the spiritual dimension of our hylomorphic humanity. But faith can and must play a role in *both* dimensions. If we believe that God wants us to perfect our bodies as well as our souls,

[28] *ST*, II-II, Q. 4, art. 7.

we must rely on faith to help us reject secular, hedonistic values and to tend to our bodies with a higher purpose in mind.

When guided by faith, we will seek *not* to glorify man and cultivate pleasure, but to glorify God and cultivate virtue. In so doing — and this is an ironic blow to the hedonists — we will also thereby be "loving our bodies" and thus maximizing our humanity in the truest sense (for more, see St. Thomas's upcoming comments on charity). We will also derive pleasure — but as a happy consequence of our fitness endeavors, rather than their ultimate end.

The gift of faith, when fully embraced, inspires us to transform our bodies and souls into powerful dynamos at the service of God and neighbor. Faith helps us rejoice in the fact that we are wondrously made by God, and wondrously gifted with the capacity to transform and perfect ourselves.

Hope for Health and Happiness

Hope describes our ardent desire for eternal life with God and our trust that he will provide us with the means to attain it. It includes the recognition that we cannot rely solely upon our own strength, but must be open to the help of the grace of the Holy Spirit. Hope addresses our aspiration for happiness, the ultimate and everlasting happiness that God will provide in the kingdom of heaven. Hope encourages us and buoys our spirits. It helps us to withdraw our focus from ourselves and motivates us to charitable actions toward our neighbors, as God has instructed us.

In our quest for bodily perfection, we must trust in God and hope that good results will come from our efforts. We must realize that God has built into our natures the means to improve ourselves, both in the ability of our faculty of reason to grasp the fundamental principles of training and diet, and in the body's physiological capacities for adaptation and growth.

I still can't help being amazed at how I can come into the gym one week and master a poundage that stopped me cold the week before, or run a given distance at a slightly faster clip. In fact, it amazes me even more that as I grow older, my body retains this capacity, not only for recuperation, but also for supercompensation by increasing strength in response to intense exercise. In midlife and beyond, we can still exercise hope for measurable physical improvement!

Indeed, I invite you to ponder a spiritual dimension of total fitness training that we haven't emphasized before. God has graced us with a wonderful gift *in the very ability to shape and build our own bodily temples:* to turn the "word" of strength-training wisdom into our own muscular flesh. We cannot create ourselves. That's God's job, of course. However, he has bestowed upon us the powers to alter, enhance, and perfect who we are, both in body and in spirit. This is an awesome and exhilarating power and responsibility. Perhaps it is merely the slightest foretaste of the bodily perfection that awaits us in our glorified state when our souls and our bodies will function truly as one. God gives us ample reason to hope for our personal perfection and happiness, both in this life and in the life to come.

Charity Forms Hylomorphic Harmony

Do you recall the *auriga virtutum?* Prudence or practical wisdom is the "charioteer of the virtues" because this unique blend of intellectual and moral virtue guides the other virtues. It helps derive practical means for achieving virtuous ends. Still, how do Christians determine which goals or ends are truly virtuous? Do you recall the *ordo caritas?* The "order of charity" sets charity or love as the ultimate ordering principle. The *Catechism* tells us that charity is "the form of all the virtues," "the source and goal of

Christian practice" that "upholds and purifies our ability to love, and raises it to the perfection of divine love."[29]

When Jesus told us that the greatest commandments are to love God with all our hearts and our neighbors as ourselves, he commanded us to exercise charity. God infuses the virtue of charity into the hearts of the faithful, and it is up to us to practice it and to live by it.

Charity, then, sets the goals and standards for every virtue, including the virtues of fitness. What is charity like, and how do we express it? St. Paul famously tells us in the thirteenth chapter of his first letter to the Corinthians what charity is and what it is not. Charity *is* patient, kind, rejoices in right, bears all things, believes all things, hopes all things, and endures all things. Charity *is not* jealous, boastful, arrogant, rude, insistent upon its own way, irritable or resentful, and does not rejoice at wrong.

"The principal act of charity," says St. Thomas, "is to love."[30] Further, he tells us, "out of the love of charity with which we love God, we ought to love our bodies also."[31]

So, too, then, must charity guide and inform our pursuit of the virtues of fitness. As we grow in physical prowess, we must train our bodies as instruments of charitable works. We must be kind to others, be patient with ourselves as we slowly progress, show joy in our successes, maintain hope in future progress, and display the fortitude to persevere in our training and diet. We should use our strength for good deeds and invite others by our words and our examples to share in the fitness lifestyle, with humility and without rude arrogance.

[29] CCC, par. 1827.
[30] *ST*, II-II, Q. 27.
[31] *ST*, II-II, Q. 25, art. 6.

Charity "binds together everything in perfect harmony." The virtue of charity integrates and enhances every part of our lives. Charity, although the greatest virtue, is also the most simple and practical. Charity does good works! We can see it with our own eyes. We express Christian love most fully through our actions, not merely our intentions. In a life ordered by charity, all of our daily actions work together in a meaningful and loving whole. Charity will not permit our fitness pursuits to steal precious time and energy from other important responsibilities to God and our neighbors. Charity does not breed self-absorption or plant discord within families.

I believe the training and dietary principles I've given you are in keeping with the order of charity. They are conducive to harmony of body and soul, and to a balanced home and spiritual life. *Brief* and *infrequent* workouts should leave you ample time for the sundry other duties and responsibilities in your life. *Eating reasonable quantities of normal foods* makes no new demands on your time or your family budget. Incorporating *household tasks* and *yard work* as methods of weight control will go far toward a happy and organized home life. The easy application of these principles *to everyone, from the youngest of the teens all the way to Grandma and Grandpa,* means you can make fitness training a family affair. *Incorporating prayer, meditation, and spiritual reading* into your lifting and exercise-bike time will help keep your spirit fed and will stoke the fires of charity within your heart.

Make Yourself Charity's Home

The Temple in Jerusalem was the place where Charity himself dwelt, and every aspect of its structure was designed to give him the utmost reverence and respect: it was beautifully crafted, built to withstand the weathering of the ages, and lovingly maintained.

You are that same Temple.

Total fitness invokes all the virtues, but above all else, it's about making a strong and beautiful home for Charity to live in, and to radiate from. Only then can we, by God's grace, answer the call to "be perfect" by loving him with all our being, and allow ourselves to be transformed by Charity and be made fit to be called his sons and daughters; fit for our inheritance of glory; fit for eternal life.

MUSCLE MASTERY TIPS AND FACTS #17

Further Reading on the Virtues of Fitness

The acquisition of virtues: Go to the *Summa Theologica* (*Second Part*), Aristotle's *Nichomachean Ethics*, and St. Thomas Aquinas's *Commentary on Aristotle's Nichomachean Ethics*.

Exercise: My knowledge of strength training comes primarily from the writings of Nautilus inventor Arthur Jones, the prolific Ellington Darden, and the late Mike Mentzer, Mr. Universe. For aerobic exercise, check out Kenneth Cooper's aerobics books, as well as *Fit or Fat*, by Covert Bailey.

Diet: An excellent book that I chanced upon while writing this one is *The Weigh Down Diet*, by Christian nutritionist Gwen Shamblin. A comprehensive college text I've found helpful for decades for its sensible and scientific approach to eating is *The Realities of Nutrition*, by Ronald Deutsch.

The total fitness package: Nobody puts the total fitness package together quite like Clarence Bass. I've been highly influenced by all of his books. *Lean for Life* is my favorite, and *Challenge Yourself* even features an iron-pumping priest. Bass's website, www.cbass.com, keeps me up to date on the world of strength training, aerobics, nutrition, leanness, and health. I also return time and again to Bryant Stamford and Porter Shimer's *Fitness Without Exercise*, a wise guide to health and fitness through sensible activity and eating.

Spirituality and fitness: Robert Feeney's *A Catholic Perspective: Physical Exercise and Sports* contains plenty of scriptural and theological insights, and it introduced me to the lean, athletic wisdom of Pope Pius XII and Pope John Paul II.

Afterword

An Ode to the Virtues of Fitness

Perfect your humanity,
And let virtues guide your way.
Robust health and sanity,
Will blossom as you work and play.
Humbleness, not vanity,
Will grow inside you day by day.

Steel your will with fortitude,
Lift weights with high intensity.
Strengthening your attitude,
And enduring propensity,
To show love and gratitude,
With muscular immensity!

Temperance shall strengthen too,
Grasp the reins, control your diet.
Gluttony do not pursue,
Stomach grumblings soon grow quiet.
Rock-hard abs and slim thighs too,
Will be yours, if you live by it.

Let justice burn in your soul,
A moral virtue, right and fair.

Fit for Eternal Life

Give what is due to young and old,
May grace-filled women have their share.
All of us, we have our role,
To make the excellent less rare.

Prudently lay out your week,
To build your temple, eat and train.
A golden mean, we do seek,
Deficiency and excess drain.
Striving for that pious peak,
Muscular virtues, we'll attain.

Just as Milo lifts his calf,
Pump iron with sincerity.
Walk, run, pray, eat right, and laugh,
Make vice like sloth a rarity.
Oh, what shoulders you shall have!
And lo, faith, hope, and charity!

Appendix

Justice:
Giving Specific Groups Their Due

"Justice is a habit whereby
a man renders to each one his due."
St. Thomas Aquinas

Appendix A

Perfecting the Feminine Form

"The human body is in its own right,
God's masterpiece in the order of visible creation."
Pope Pius XII

"This at last is bone of my bones and flesh of my flesh;
she shall be called Woman."
Genesis 2:23

The fundamental principles of strength training, aerobic exercise, and balanced nutrition apply to just about everybody, whether man, woman, and child (over the age of twelve or so). It goes without saying that fortitude and temperance are a must for us all as well; for virtues are fundamental to perfecting our *human* natures.

But God did create us *man and woman*. And although many principles apply to both, in more or less equal measure, women do have certain particular needs and considerations that ought to be addressed separately. Especially if we wish (and I do) to give full credit to the specially complex and wonderful way that God designed the female body.

The Glorified Female Body

The human body, both in male and female form, is indeed God's masterpiece (would God have taken one for himself if it weren't?). He gave us our bodies as instruments to express the powers and capacities of our souls. Men and women share these powers in common, although their bodies differ in some respects. Men, of course, tend to be stronger, especially in the upper body, because of our greater quantities of the masculinizing hormone testosterone. Women tend to be better adapted, pound for pound, for lower-body strength and for some endurance activities, because of their tendency to have wider hips and narrower shoulders, providing a strong base for movement without excessive upper-body mass to lug around. Of course, part of the reason for the woman's unique advantages goes back to that most special of powers that God gives only to them: the capacity to bear and give birth to children.

Women and men will not cease to be women and men in their glorified heavenly state; it follows, then, that both are called to become perfect — not only as human beings, but as female and male human beings specifically. If you're a woman, it's fitting, therefore, for you to perfect your temple of the Holy Spirit and to glorify God with your body in a particularly *womanly* way (although not in the way the world tries to steer you — toward a narrowly defined "ideal" body shape designed to fit the fashion of the hour). You will strive, like men, to become leaner and stronger, but you won't be seeking mannish levels of strength, muscularity, and body fat.

Let's take a look at some special concerns that women face as they pursue that goal.

Hold the Massive Muscles, Please

Some women never try strength training for fear that they'll wake up someday looking like Arnold Schwarzenegger. Well, don't worry. After all, there are thousands upon thousands of men out there *trying* their best to look like The Governator, but it just ain't happening. Although men and women both have testosterone, the hormone that stimulates muscular growth, men have far higher levels of it. So, most women (and many men) couldn't build huge muscles if they tried.

Still, the inborn propensity toward muscular mass does vary from individual to individual, and it is possible (although unlikely) that you could do strength training and end up with some muscle mass you'd rather not have. Some women may have the propensity for developing rather large muscles especially in the thighs, calves, hips, and gluteus maximus. If you're a woman doing strength training, you might even notice that when first embarking on this total fitness regimen, your pants are fitting even tighter around the hips and thighs. But please don't kick strength training out the door on this account.

Consider first that muscle growth can be controlled and even reversed to some extent by reducing intensity. If you should find yourself developing unwanted muscle mass in the lower body, lighten the weights and increase the repetitions, moving perhaps from a fairly heavy weight for eight to twelve repetitions to a lighter weight for fifteen to twenty-five repetitions. You could also cut back on the intensity and increase the duration on aerobic exercises that can lead to leg mass, such as bicycling or stair-climbing machines.

Further, bear in mind that although your muscles start to grow fairly quickly in response to strength training, the combination of strength training, aerobic exercise, and proper nutrition will also work to gradually reduce your fat stores — both the fat you store outside your muscles under the skin, and that fat marbling the muscle tissue. Hence, a thigh that might show a slight increase in size initially in response to this training will become *smaller* over time. And remember, muscle requires more calories at rest than does fat. Those muscles you build will serve as future fat-burning engines.

You see, for women, too, intense strength training of the body's skeletal muscles is more important than aerobic exercise in perfecting bodily form and function. In fact, because women naturally have less muscle mass, a different distribution of body-fat storage, and smaller bones than men, one could argue that *strength training is even more important for women than it is for men.*

But wait, there's more!

On Cellulite and Sagging Skin

Another common concern among women is cellulite, and again, the hip, buttocks, and thigh areas are the target zones. Whereas men tend to store fat first in their abdominal regions, women tend to store fat around the hips, butt, and thighs (here's the "different distribution of body-fat storage" just mentioned). The skin tends to be pulled taut around guys' "beer bellies." (Some men who look almost pregnant will even brag that you can still see their "abs" — unaware that the fat underneath their abdominal sheath is actually forcing those muscles outward.) The fat that women tend to gather in the hips and thighs, however, has a tendency to produce those unwanted little cottage-cheese-like dimples called cellulite.

In Roger Schwab's excellent book on high-intensity training for women (*The Strength of a Woman*), he tells of an experiment involving three women with cellulite. The first underwent liposuction, the second used a purported "reducing cream," and the third did a circuit of strength-training exercises for three weeks. The cream did nothing. The liposuction reduced fat and overall size, but the cellulite remained. Only the woman who did strength training showed a significant decrease in cellulite — such that the other two took up strength training themselves. Why? Because larger, firmer muscles made her skin tauter, thus flattening out the dimples. And the same principle can apply to the sagging skin that can come from excessive weight loss. When skin looks loose and saggy after weight loss, it is due in part to the loss of muscle tissue. Muscle built through strength training is again the key to keeping our skin as taut and firm as it can be.

Yes, Bone's About It

Another benefit of strength training is that it tends to thicken the bones, making them less susceptible to the mineral depletion that spurs osteoporosis (bone loss) and can lead to unwanted fractures later in life. Women are more susceptible to this problem than men, partly because their bones tend to be smaller and thinner in the first place. Benefits may be realized throughout your life span, but they'll be maximized by starting strength training early, even in the teenage years. Later in life, strength training may also have some beneficial effects in preventing and alleviating arthritis, as the motions encourage the flow of synovial fluids in and out of the joints.

The Muscle-Savvy Mother

Here's another benefit that caring mothers may receive from understanding and practicing total fitness training. As I'll detail further two chapters down the road, the popular media are feeding your teenage sons and daughters some very dangerous messages both about how their bodies "should" look, and about how they should eat and exercise to achieve that look. They might be surprised, shocked, alarmed (and maybe even grateful someday) if Mom is able to talk to them about diet and exercise with some measure of authority, having practiced what she's preached. Who knows? Your son may even be amazed to see that you can explain the fundamentals of pumping iron better than some of the muscle-heavy (and brain-light) guys hanging out at the gym all day!

Form Follows Function

Let's re-examine some advice from an avid swimmer, fitness advocate — and pope. Pope Pius XII noted, as we saw at the beginning of this chapter, that the human body is, in its own right, God's masterpiece of creation. Further, as we saw at the start of chapter 1, he said the Church is all for physical culture, if it be in proper proportion.

All right, we are wondrously made. We can be thankful that we've been blessed with our physical bodies. We all possess physical beauty deriving from the fact that we were crafted "in God's image." We need not look like Hercules or Aphrodite. We can be satisfied with who we are while we strive to improve within our own unique, individual God-given limits. And let's not lose sight of that "proper proportion." We should not fall prey to the "cult of the body." We must remember the mind and the spirit as well. Our bodies are our instruments, not our masters.

Unfortunately, our culture encourages women very early on to base too much of their self-worth on how they look, over-valuing physical beauty that is only skin deep, and under-valuing the mind and spirit. Let proper total fitness training help buck that trend. Even within the realm of the physical, one way to do this is to focus more on function, and less on form; more on what you can do, less on how you look; more on feeling good, less on looking good. Experience the delight of gaining strength, of carrying the babies or the groceries with greater ease than before, of playing sports with the family without becoming winded, of performing more tirelessly on the job.

Even so, recall happily that form tends to follow function. Muscles get bigger, for example, when they're made stronger. As your strength and endurance build, you'll also find yourself more pleased with your figure. And so will God, whose glory will be magnified in the beautiful perfection of his creatures.

MUSCLE MASTERY TIPS AND FACTS #18

A Woman's Place Is in the Gym?

When Pro-Form Fitness Center opened in Springfield, Illinois, in the late 1970s, it was the only serious weight-lifting gym in town, outside of the YMCA, and in its first year of existence, it did not even have a locker room for women. Well, times soon changed. A few years later, the local Nautilus fitness center went out of business, and Pro-Form bought its equipment and incorporated its members. This produced an interesting combination of hardcore iron-pumping muscle heads and more normal folks interested in health and fitness, many of them women. By that time, Pro-Form had a women's locker room, and today, what large commercial gym doesn't? Growing numbers of women have realized that strength training is not for men only. Particularly popular among women are various kinds of group exercise involving forms of aerobic or mild strength training. These, too, can be included in your fitness regimen, if they are your cup of tea. (I'm a coffee man myself.) And speaking of tea, I happened to meet one of the biggest tea drinkers I know at a gym. I have been her fitness instructor since 1983 (and her husband since 1984).

Appendix B

Use It or Lose It!

"For what utterance can be more pitiable than that of Milo of Crotona? After he was already an old man and was watching the athletes training in the racecourse, it is related that as he looked upon his shrunken muscles, he wept and said: 'Yes, but now they are dead.' "

Cicero

"But it is our duty, my young friends, to resist old age; to compensate for its defects by a watchful care; to fight against it as we would fight against disease; to adopt a regimen of health; to practice moderate exercise; and to take just enough of food and drink to restore our strength and not to overburden it. Nor indeed are we to give our attention solely to the body; much greater care is due to the mind and soul; for they, too, like lamps, grow dim with time, unless we keep them supplied with oil."

Cicero

Over the passage of time, our bodies suffer significant decline in virtually every system: from the musculoskeletal to the cardiovascular, from the respiratory to the digestive, from the urological to the neurological. And we're only too aware of how our hair changes color (or goes away), our skin loses its suppleness, our joints ache, and our muscles shrink.

Now, some of this decline is inevitable, of course. (After all, there are no Methusalehs among us anymore.) Some people, therefore, advocate an approach to aging that involves a gradual withdrawal from the responsibilities and activities of one's younger years — fearful perhaps of wearing out already-creaking limbs. But although there's something to be said for spending our later years in relaxed contemplation and repose, when it comes to maintenance of both physical and mental capacities, I say, "Use it or lose it!" And indeed, scientific studies show that elderly individuals who follow Cicero's advice (second quotation at the beginning of this chapter) do tend to retain more of their muscular and mental capacities than their more disengaged peers. Although we can't reverse the physical effects of the Fall (that will come at the resurrection), we *can* take special, proactive measures to counteract some of those effects, and maintain a high level of fitness and strength well into our golden years.

Along the way, we would be well-advised to keep in mind that old prayer sometimes attributed to St. Francis: "God grant me the strength to change the things I can change, the patience to accept the things I cannot change, and the wisdom to know the difference." How do we acquire the wisdom to know what can be changed and what cannot? In two ways. One is to familiarize yourself with research in the field of gerontology — and I'll share some with you in this chapter — and the second is to thoughtfully, carefully, and prayerfully put various fitness practices to the test *on yourself*.

Cicero reminds us that our lamps grow dim without oil. In this chapter, let's see what we can do to put fuel in our lamps (and make sure that they're never blotted out under the baskets of our own inactivity).

Milo and Me

Milo of Croton, you'll recall from chapter 3, was the greatest of the ancient Olympic athletes and the Father of Progressive Resistance. His story was so fabulously triumphant, yet it took a tragic turn in midlife. When Milo was forty-five, he withdrew from wrestling competition, realizing that the toll of years had left him unable to defeat one Timastitheos, possibly his own pupil. From that point until his death at fifty-seven, Milo went into sad decline. Just imagine the once-incomparable Milo staring down at flabby limbs, declining even to help his youthful admirers, feeling no longer physically worthy. If that's not tragic enough, consider one version of the end of his life, in which Milo, walking alone, tested his remaining strength by prying apart two halves of a tree trunk partially split by some woodcutters, whereupon the halves sprung back and his hands were trapped. Unable to free himself, Milo was devoured by hungry wolves!

The take-home message for me, when I realized I had reached that same declining age of forty-five, was simple: don't be another Milo! With the advances in exercise science and nutrition in our modern times, I knew there was no reason to go totally downhill at forty-five. On the contrary, I viewed it as a challenge to *begin* to get into the best shape of my life. I was sure that I had the *knowledge* I needed to get myself into tip-top shape. But did I have the will and the discipline — without which, as Aristotle and St. Thomas had taught me well, the virtue of fitness was impossible? Milo didn't have it.[32]

Our lesson for this chapter, then, is that you're never too old to make some kind of improvement — even a dramatic one — in your quest for physical, mental, and spiritual perfection.

Temple Maintenance: From Youth to Middle Age

Some of our bodily organs begin their gradual steady decline in peak performance even in our twenties. Still, the majority of decline in form and function that most of us see in our thirties and forties has far more to do with our habits than with our physiology. Consider the typical man who is fairly active in his high school and college days, settles into a sedentary lifestyle in early adulthood, and finds himself a good twenty pounds heavier in his forties. This is a very common scenario, and it is actually *worse* than it appears. Those twenty pounds, you see, mean that he's probably packing an extra *thirty* pounds of blubber! You see, his sedentary lifestyle has cost him ten pounds of muscle. Even in young adulthood, the "use it or lose it" principle applies to our muscle mass, and many of us may go years without worrying as our body weights stay relatively stable, while all the time muscle is wasting away and being replaced with unseemly and unhealthy fat.

---

[32] Continuing the passage I quoted earlier, Cicero went on to assault Milo's character, chiding, "You never gained renown for your real self, but from brute strength of lungs and limb."

This trend can be halted and reversed in middle age by the principles of diet and exercise I've given you. Men's testosterone levels typically stay high at least until the mid-fifties, allowing them to maintain near-peak strength and muscle mass. Women, too, can reverse this common trend. And they should: the sedentary lifestyle of early and mid-adulthood sets the stage for both sexes for many diseases, from hypertension to diabetes, arthritis, and osteoporosis. Striving for total fitness may help to prevent them or at least to mitigate their negative effects.

But even after midlife, it isn't too late to halt and partially reverse the toll of years of inactivity and overeating. Let's look next at a small sample of research findings gleaned from formal strength-training studies with normal elderly adult men and women.

Fitness Among the Elderly: The Research

As I mentioned earlier, a huge body of research has accrued in the field of gerontology that supports the "use it or lose it" approach. Just a few hours ago, my Internet home page featured an article on five ways to reduce your risk of Alzheimer's disease (this piqued my interest because my doctoral dissertation was on the neuropsychology of early Alzheimer's dementia). The top two involved exercise. Number one was *exercise your mind* (once again, Cicero's right on target). Number two was *exercise your body*.

Let me give you a small taste of what modern scientific research on total fitness and the elderly, published in such journals as the *Journal of Gerontology: Medical Sciences*, has taught us:

• Grip strength tends to decline after age twenty, but with training, it may remain stable to age sixty or beyond.

• High grip strength in middle-age men predicts a lower chance of premature death.

• Muscle mass makes us better able to recuperate from trauma in middle and later life.

• Active elderly women may function as well as inactive women a decade younger.

• Leg-press power translates into higher capacity for functions of daily living among elderly women.

• Single-set high-intensity strength training stimulates retention of bone mass among men ages sixty to seventy-five.

• Elderly men can show improvement in single-repetition strength, multi-repetition strength, aerobic capacity, blood lipids, and muscle-cell size with brief, infrequent, high-intensity training to failure.

The lesson here is clear: A good deal of the loss in strength and endurance that was thought to come inevitably with aging is really a matter of *disuse*, and can be partially reversed. Those of us who are to pay our dues by training for total fitness will also be the most likely to remain most functional as the years go by, and to enjoy ourselves the most in the process.

And let me point out that modest gains in strength, such as those highlighted in the bullet points earlier, can make a lot of real-world difference later in life. The middle-aged couch potato may not be pleased by his shrinking legs and expanding middle, but he can still walk around under his own power. Consider the eighty-year-old with serious disuse muscle atrophy, perhaps due to fractures from osteoporotic bones that could have been thickened through years of weight-bearing exercise. To him or her, the simple ability to stand and walk unassisted may seem like wishing for the moon. Strength training, ideally throughout the lifespan but even when adopted late in life, may make the difference in making possible those normal daily activities that younger people take for granted.

Age-Appropriate Goal Setting

Goals are what motivate us to achieve; in our case, to get lean and strong, and to acquire virtue. Realistic goal-setting — adapted to our age and condition — is doubly crucial as we enter middle age and beyond. As the years roll on by, the once-youthful weightlifter who thought of nothing but adding another five pounds to the bar may find himself enjoying moving a little lighter weight, with a lot better form, as a part of a balanced total fitness program. We must become wiser and more careful in our training as we mature. We may become more susceptible to injury, and we may require a little more time for rest and recuperation.

In our twenties and thirties, Mike (my main weightlifting partner since 1983) and I used to joke during each workout that we were going to train "whatever muscles weren't injured," but in our middle-age years, we find ourselves seldom injured anymore. Part of the reason, I believe, is one of the adjustments we've made: we have moved away from barbells and dumbbells and toward strength-training machines. This has really worked for us. (I address some of the general pros and cons of free weights versus machines in Muscle Mastery Tips and Facts #8.) By adapting our workouts this way, Mike and I have been able to keep our intensity high, and keep our injuries — at an age when we're more susceptible — to a minimum.

Wisdom: Age's Timeless Virtue

Still, many of us will live to see the day when, despite our most diligent efforts, our physical temples will see some unavoidable decline. But even then, as beings of body and soul, we can continue to play important roles in the realm of total fitness. Consider again Milo's folly. Rather than wallowing in self-pity about his flabby limbs, perhaps he could have reached out to those youths and shared with them the athletic wisdom that comes only from age and experience. A person of true strength and moral fortitude exerts his strength not only for his own benefit, but for that of his neighbor. And if his bodily strength should wane, he will strive to compensate all the more through charitably sharing his wisdom and strength of character.

MUSCLE MASTERY TIPS AND FACTS #19

Take This Pill with Water

I'm using the word *pill* metaphorically. Think about strength and aerobic training as powerful medicines. They can work wonders, but only in the right dosage, for you. And just as with other pills, you need to take exercise with plenty of water. Drink plenty of fluids, especially before and after aerobic exercise and especially during warm weather. But don't obsess about it. Water obtained through sodas, milk, tea, coffee, juice, and even water-logged foods such as fruit also help keep us hydrated. Some people give water almost magical significance with regard to weight loss. They drink gallons of water per day, stretching their stomachs along the way. But remember: moderation. Let your thirst guide you.

For the Young

Help Your Training
Teen Avoid the Pitfalls

"Odysseus tucked up his rags round his middle and bared his great and shapely thighs. His broad shoulders too, and his chest and brawny arms now caught the eye. Indeed Athena herself intervened to increase his royal stature. As a result, all the suitors were lost in amazement, and significant glances and comments were exchanged."

Homer

"For I shall not be a Milo, either, and yet I do not neglect my body . . . nor, in a word, is there any field in which we give up the appropriate discipline merely from despair of attaining the highest."

Epictetus

"Rejoice, O young man, in your youth."

Ecclesiastes 11:9

When it comes to perfecting their temples of the Holy Spirit, there are so many reasons for both young men and women to rejoice in their youth. The physical changes of early adolescence are not without their awkward moments, but nonetheless, when boys and girls reach their teens, they're entering a very special time for maximizing their strength and endurance, perfecting their youthful muscles, hearts, and lungs, and setting the stage for a lifetime of physical and spiritual vigor.

Yet, unfortunately, in our modern culture, teens are growing obese at higher rates than ever. Diseases following obesity, such as diabetes, are also on the upswing among our youths. This is all so unnecessary for boys and girls who can apply the strength- and endurance-training principles in this book with maximum effect. Do you recall our discussion about the delicate interplay between proper doses of intense exercise and proper rest? Well, healthy adolescents, with their peak recuperative powers, can handle *stronger* doses and get by with *less* rest than we older folks can. *Adolescents are at their peak capacity for squeezing maximum results from their training, especially in the later teenage years.* Further, they're at the ideal time of life for the acquisition of habits of "muscular virtue" that can serve them for the rest of their lives. So get them off the couch! As we are told in Proverbs, "Train up a child in the way he should go: and when he is old, he will not depart from it."[33]

[33] Prov. 22:6.

Parents' Role and Grandma's Law

This, of course, is our job as parents. We already ardently seek to train our children in the Faith and in the moral life. A growing number of Christian parents are schooling their children at home, too. I believe it's no less important for parents to train children in the ways that will glorify God through the proper use and perfection of their bodies. If we can inculcate in them a deeply ingrained sense of the body as the temple of the Holy Spirit, one that will permeate their thoughts about the body and the daily actions that flow from those thoughts, we will have done them a great service in many ways. It will help spare them from hurtful dichotomous thinking that acknowledges things of the spirit as the realm of the Church, but forfeits things of the body to the prevailing modern secular messages.

We need to drive home fully the message of how we are integrated hylomorphic creatures, and how whatever we do with our bodies affects our souls. We must teach them to treat the body with respect and seek to perfect it. Children who grow up imbued with the idea of "body as temple" will be much less likely to be swayed by peers who would introduce them to dangerous, unhealthful, or immoral behaviors.

We can train children in this way by teaching them about exercise and diet, and their spiritual context, and also by example and encouragement. Every parent knows that every child is born with his own unique temperament and personality. Not every child is going to want to be a competitive weightlifter or runner, nor should he. But the basic activities of some form of strength and endurance training (at the least through healthy forms of normal physical labor) are of value for *everybody*. We need to exhort our children to find joy in healthy physical activities, however simple.

My older son came to the gym with me for a while at about age thirteen, but it just wasn't the thing for him. Neither did he enjoy running. Still, he and his friends came to love playing basketball and golf and tennis. He mowed neighbors' lawns, ate sensibly, and stayed lean and healthy. Then, at nineteen, he regained a desire to get back to the gym for strength training. You see, his brother, six years his younger, had gotten "bitten by the iron bug." He loved working out, and this motivated his older brother to stay ahead of the little squirt, of course. Now, at times, the whole family does strength training together.

To put the principles of physical and spiritual fitness to practice with our youths of today, we must again go back to wise old Aristotle and his focus on *moderation*, both with regard to those things youths should do more frequently, and to those they should do *less* often. One of the fitness scourges of today's youths is overindulgence in video games. I fear that we're producing children with very lean and muscular thumbs connected to bodies unconditioned like never before.

If you have these games in your house, and kids who spend too much time in front of them, I suggest using a psychological technique called the Premack Principle (also known as "Grandma's law") which is simply, "First you work, then you play." Let a time-limited game session of perhaps an hour or so follow more vigorous and healthful activities.

The Personal Fable
"They have exalted notions, because they have not been humbled by life or learned its necessary limitations . . . Their lives are regulated more by feeling than by reasoning . . . all their mistakes are in the direction of doing things excessively and vehemently."

Do these words of Aristotle's ring true to you, in your daily struggle to raise teenagers? The exalted notions and excessive behaviors of youths have been around a long time indeed.

If you can remember your own adolescent years, you probably feel that you were *unique* in the world. Sure, everybody is an individual, but you were, well, *you*, and not like other people. Who could possibly understand your thoughts? Who had ever thought or felt such things before? Certainly, not, of all people, your parents (apparently *born* adults, they were). And then there was your own unique, *special destiny*. How could others understand that the limitations that apply to other people really weren't valid for you? Perhaps you felt well-nigh *invincible* at times.

Modern psychologist David Elkind notes how some of these thought processes and reckless behaviors arise from an adolescent egocentrism, or a tendency to see the world only through one's own perspective. This is the idea of the *personal fable*: an overblown sense of uniqueness and special destiny that can lead to feelings of invincibility — and thus give rise to the dangerous risky behaviors of adolescence. Also common is the sense of the *imaginary audience*, the feeling that one's self is the focus of everyone else's attention. This may explain some of the power of peer pressure in adolescence. (Perhaps one of the great rewards of growing up is the realization that most people are actually a little too engrossed in their own concerns to spend all day thinking about yours!)

Seven years ago, I conducted a survey among adults pursuing certification as personal fitness trainers, and I found that most of them (myself included) had seriously embraced a dandy of a personal fable in our own teen years. Several of us were convinced that we would become Mr. Olympia, holder of the loftiest bodybuilding title reserved for only the greatest of Mr. Universe winners. Only ten men alive at the time had won that title, so, with a world population of around six billion and roughly one-half of them males, Mr. Olympias were about a one-in-300-million phenomenon; yet several of us were pretty darn confident that the greatest set of muscles in all the world would be our own.

Personal fables can be amusing when we have survived them and can look back on them with perspectives wisened by experience. But in the world of fitness training, they truly can spell danger for some adolescent boys. If a boy is fired with the idea that he can excel at a world-class level in some sport, if he feels a sense of special destiny and invincibility, of imperviousness to harm, and at the same time, he feels all eyes are upon him, he may be willing to take foolhardy risks to pursue that personal pipe dream. His behaviors may far exceed the mean of manly fortitude and lead him headlong into reckless and foolhardy excesses. In the world of strength training and athletics, these excesses include steroid abuse, overtraining, excessive use of food supplements, and dieting extremes.

Harmful Hazards: Steroids, Creatine, and Bulking Up

Anabolic steroids are manmade, synthetic versions of the male hormone testosterone. They're anabolic and androgenic, which means they induce growth and they induce male secondary sexual characteristics. They're usually taken in pill form or injected, although other forms, such as creams or formulas that dissolve under the tongue, are also out there. They're illegal and quite detrimental to physical (let alone mental and spiritual) perfection. An adolescent using steroids will get bigger and stronger while he uses them, but at the peril of long-term damage to his liver, his heart, and other body organs and systems. Further, he will be more susceptible to muscle, ligament, tendon, and bone damage as his body becomes capable of exerting forces beyond its own structural integrity.

Minor visible side effects include facial bloating and puffiness and facial and bodily acne. More serious side effects may follow. For example, both men and women have testosterone and estrogen (a feminizing hormone) in their systems. When a male takes steroids, his body compensates by reducing his own natural supply of testosterone, so that, for a period after steroids are discontinued, the balance has tilted more to the estrogen side, and so males may actually develop breast tissue (removable, perhaps, only through surgery). Steroids are bad news, and parents who note their adolescent males making tremendous, sudden gains in size and strength would do well to talk to them about steroids.

Another substance that can produce fairly substantial gains in size and strength is *creatine*. It's not a steroid, but a substance found naturally in some foods, especially meats, that provides energy for muscles. Creatine may explain, to some extent, the widespread idea of "meat for strength" prevalent even back to the days of Milo. I must say, it's the only food supplement I've ever seen that actually seems to work, with almost steroid-like effects. Yet even here, there may be pitfalls. I suffered partial biceps tears on two separate occasions when I was using the substance. (Neither injury occurred during high-intensity strength training, by the way. One happened during a tennis serve, and another as I was tugging against a ski-boat engine while trying to learn to wakeboard.) I haven't seen scientific research on this, but I've heard others, including medical doctors, attribute their muscular injuries to creatine use, too.

Creatine can lead to weight gain, and it may contribute to bloating the body with water. (Muscle itself, remember, is about 70 percent water.) This may be hard on some people's kidneys. Some individuals are also prone to muscle cramps while using this substance. It happened to me. Personally, I don't find creatine worth the risk, expense, and bother for an adult, let alone for the adolescent male who is brimming over with natural growth-producing male hormone as it is. But this hasn't stopped it from finding its way into high schools all around the country.

A related potential pitfall for adolescent males is the general phenomenon of "bulking up," even if steroids or creatine are not involved. I don't believe this is as common now as it was in my day, except perhaps in the world of high school football. "Bulking up" refers to purposely becoming as huge as possible, even if much of it is fat, with the idea that one will eventually get rid of the fat and find a massively muscled body underneath. In my day, this led to practices such as drinking a gallon of whole milk each day (a good friend of mine preferred a gallon of ice cream). My bulking period actually came after a couple of years of "health food" fanaticism where I kept my diet quite pristine — working at a fast-food burger joint without tasting a sip of soda or even a hamburger bun (white bread, you know). Aristotle was right about me as a youth, as I was all about excess and vehemence! (Maybe this is why I was later so drawn to "The Man with the Golden Mean.")

Obviously, purposely bulking up in this way can make it that much harder to keep lean later in life. Plus, even young adults have been found to have early blockages of the arteries of the heart attributable to poor dietary practices earlier in life. And remember the all-so-common problem of high-volume eating we discussed in part III, on nutrition? Through bulking up, the teenage boy is actually training himself in this self-destructive habit of gluttony.

Fractured Fairy Tales

So how does the personal fable usually end? Fortunately, the vast majority of adolescents do live through those tumultuous teenage years and shut the book on the personal fable. Reality it-self has a lot to do with it. Teens who are willing to do absolutely anything to become that Mr. Olympia or Super Bowl champion, find that, try as they will, although their muscles are growing to some extent, it's nothing like they had imagined. It helps when they learn that so much of muscle building comes down to individual genetics and inborn limitations; no matter what they do, most teenagers will never become "huge." It's just not in their genes. (As Mike Mentzer put it, the most important first step in becoming a world-class bodybuilder is "choosing the right parents.") *Their* "perfect" bodily temple will take some more modest form.

When the fable bursts, one risk is that the adolescent male will give up training altogether. This is even more likely if he had bought into the concept that strength training means hours and hours of volume training. There's that dichotomous "all or noth-ing" thinking so antithetical to virtue and the golden mean, and this is where I direct your attention back to the quotation from Epictetus. Epictetus knows he can be no Milo, yet he doesn't ne-glect his body. He can still perfect and improve Epictetus. Indeed, Epictetus himself was known for having a lame leg, but it doesn't seem to have slowed him down much.

Teenage Girls: Is Thin Still In?

While boys hear the call, both from the media and from them-selves, that "bigger is better," girls are still being told and shown that "thin is in." For every image of a heavily muscled professional male athlete to inspire young boys, we seem to find an emaciated fashion model or movie actress to provide girls an image of what they should be.

If I may be allowed to exaggerate just a bit, imagine this not-too-farfetched scene. Mom is driving the family van. Her son and his buddy in one bank of seats, and her daughter and her friend in another, are discussing what they had for lunch that day. Her son and his buddy regale each other with stories of multi-layer bacon cheeseburgers washed down with extra-large chocolate shakes, while her daughter and her friend discuss their lunches of lettuce-and-air salads.

Think back to the section on giving women their due. In comparison with the male body, the female body was designed with important similarities and important differences. What could be more obvious and wonderful? Where the male's broad shoulders work well for pushing and shoving and hitting and throwing, the female's narrower, rounder, and softer form is very well adapted for drawing in, for holding, for comforting and soothing. And yet, while media images, in sports, music, and movies, glorify exaggerated hard masculine characteristics — power, aggressiveness, all of those "warrior" qualities — they tend to ignore or denigrate the wonderful and truly feminine characteristics.

Ideal body types change with the times, but doesn't it seem for a long time that bodies of *fashion models* have resembled those of skinny prepubescent boys — exceedingly narrow, thin, and shapeless, noticeably lacking in feminine curves? Studies have shown that as real American women have become a little heavier over recent decades, models and pageant winners have become both lighter and taller, creating greater and greater distance between the real and the ideal. Is this "ideal" really what we want for our daughters? Especially considering the obsession with body shape that it inspires — beginning now even in the early grade-school years.

In what area are the vices of deficiency and extremity more clearly illustrated than in our modern culture's approach to the female body? The beautiful people that girls see on TV and movie screens are so often dangerously thin, yet during the commercials (or up at the snack bar), those girls are being encouraged to super-size their meals.

So what should girls do? What should the parents of teenage daughters do? I think we need to work hard to broaden girls' horizons on the nature of the body and what it truly means to perfect herself in mind, body, and soul. In fitness training, this means a very conscious cultivation of balance, of striving for the mean, of nothing in excess. It also means giving her a model of total fitness based on a Christian anthropology: male and female we were created; women are meant to have softer, curvier bodies with more fat, and this is a good thing.

As I noted in the chapter on women, it's also a good thing to *focus more on function than on form.* Help the adolescent girl achieve a sense of accomplishment based on what she can do, not just on how she looks. If she improves in performance, getting a little stronger and more aerobically fit, chances are she will feel much better, and look better, too, as a pleasant side effect. She will not come to look like the models on the stage, and that is a very good thing.

Of course, in terms of both mental and spiritual fitness, Christian girls will have a huge advantage if they would learn about Mary, the Mother of God, and about other great women saints, women who accomplished meaningful and beautiful things in life, while glorifying God, helping humanity, and ignoring the messages of the secular culture that would give them false images of what it means to be a woman.

MUSCLE MASTERY TIPS AND FACTS #20

Speaking Specifically of Sports

Many adolescents may pursue total fitness to improve their performance in sports. In recent decades, the value of cross-training and strength training have become increasingly recognized in endurance sports. Be aware, though, that your exercises need not, in fact *should not*, mimic your sport. You shouldn't shoot a weighted basketball or connect a baseball to a pulley machine. It will provide a very poor strength-training stimulation, and it will throw off your coordination. I also question the value of "plyometrics," or explosive, ballistic jumping and weight-throwing exercises.

Last year, a friend of mine did a regimen of light, explosive leg presses to increase his vertical leap for basketball. It didn't help much. I gave him this analogy: "If you wanted your car to go faster in a drag race, would it be better to slam on the gas pedal as hard as you can, again and again, or to go out and get a bigger engine?" Our muscles are our engines. Their strength creates *speed*. The more weight your muscles are able to move, the more quickly they will be able to move lighter weights. This season, my friend tried an alternative. Using HIT principles, he did his leg presses slowly, and he progressed using heavier weights each workout. Just last week, he showed me the blisters he'd developed on his fingers from grabbing the basketball rim.

Biographical Note

Kevin Vost

Kevin Vost (b. 1961) is a professor of psychology, a veteran body-builder, a Mensa member, and in his spare time, a devotee of the Classics and St. Thomas Aquinas. He lives in Springfield, Illinois, with his wife and two sons.

Sophia Institute Press®

Sophia Institute® is a nonprofit institution that seeks to restore man's knowledge of eternal truth, including man's knowledge of his own nature, his relation to other persons, and his relation to God. Sophia Institute Press® serves this end in numerous ways: it publishes translations of foreign works to make them accessible for the first time to English-speaking readers; it brings out-of-print books back into print; and it publishes important new books that fulfill the ideals of Sophia Institute®. These books afford readers a rich source of the enduring wisdom of mankind.

Sophia Institute Press® makes these high-quality books available to the general public by using advanced technology and by soliciting donations to subsidize its general publishing costs. Your generosity can help Sophia Institute Press® to provide the public with editions of works containing the enduring wisdom of the ages. Please send your tax-deductible contribution to the address below. We welcome your questions, comments, and suggestions.

For your free catalog, call:
Toll-free: 1-800-888-9344

Sophia Institute Press®
Box 5284
Manchester, NH 03108
www.sophiainstitute.com

Sophia Institute® is a tax-exempt institution as defined by the Internal Revenue Code, Section 501(c)(3). Tax I.D. 22-2548708.